THE WALL THAT
FAILED

THE WALL THAT FAILED

How One Community Navigated the Shifting
Sands of Integration in West Texas

EVELYN ROSSLER STRODER

THE WALL THAT FAILED
HOW ONE COMMUNITY NAVIGATED THE SHIFTING SANDS OF INTEGRATION IN WEST TEXAS

Copyright © 2016 Evelyn Rossler Stroder.

All rights reserved. No part of this book may be used or reproduced by any means, graphic, electronic, or mechanical, including photocopying, recording, taping or by any information storage retrieval system without the written permission of the author except in the case of brief quotations embodied in critical articles and reviews.

iUniverse books may be ordered through booksellers or by contacting:

iUniverse
1663 Liberty Drive
Bloomington, IN 47403
www.iuniverse.com
1-800-Authors (1-800-288-4677)

Because of the dynamic nature of the Internet, any web addresses or links contained in this book may have changed since publication and may no longer be valid. The views expressed in this work are solely those of the author and do not necessarily reflect the views of the publisher, and the publisher hereby disclaims any responsibility for them.

Any people depicted in stock imagery provided by Thinkstock are models, and such images are being used for illustrative purposes only.
Certain stock imagery © Thinkstock.

ISBN: 978-1-5320-0398-1 (sc)
ISBN: 978-1-5320-2410-8 (hc)
ISBN: 978-1-5320-0399-8 (e)

Library of Congress Control Number: 2016915571

Print information available on the last page.

iUniverse rev. date: 09/18/2017

Before I built a wall I'd ask to know
What I was walling in or walling out,
And to whom I was like to give offence.
Something there is that doesn't love a wall,
That wants it down.

—Robert Frost, "Mending Wall"[1]

---

1 Robert Frost, "Mending Wall," in *North of Boston* by Robert Frost (New York: Henry Holt and Company, 1925), 2.

CONTENTS

Foreword ix

I. The Motivation

Chapter 1: Of Lights and a Wall 1

II. The Setting and the Characters

Chapter 2: The Ways We Were—Town Kids and Camp Kids 37
Chapter 3: The Ways We Were—Black Kids and the Hub 62

III. The Plot

Chapter 4: Opening-Day Jitters 93
Chapter 5: Growing Pains and Pleasures 110
Chapter 6: Grace under Pressure, Faith over All 127
Chapter 7: You Can Go Home Again 143
Chapter 8: Tales for Enrichment 155
Chapter 9: Universal Perplexities 195

IV. Outlooks

Chapter 10: Up a Road Slowly 209

Afterword 219
After-Afterword 225
Appendices 229
Bibliography 243
About the Author 245
Index 247
Acknowledgements and Notes 253
Author Bio 257

FOREWORD

December 3, 2011. It's the evening of the naming/dedication of a Crane, Texas, high school gym to the memory of Tommy Jones, athlete extraordinaire, person remarkable, citizen of two worlds become one in this little one-stoplight town. It's the evening I realize why this story has taken so long to finish and that its time has come.

We had to come full circle. Not to the end—that never happens with a circle—but to a pause-and-look-back place from which we can keep moving forward and expanding our circle.

It's been nearly five decades since the Jones boys and company became part of Crane's first athletic team ever to make the Texas state finals—not so coincidentally the first year of racial integration in this basic West Texas oil field town. In the fall of 1965, we had finally conformed to the US Supreme Court ruling of a decade earlier.

Tonight we celebrate Tommy as a personification of the spirit of forgiveness and getting on with life. Of the spirit of the young when a barrier they've never understood or known or cared much about is removed, at least technically.

And tonight the exuberance still bubbles almost palpably, just as it did in the 1960s.

As the young people of Tommy's day, now in the Social Security generation, chat and celebrate anew, and their Tommy stories fill the air, we all realize what a remarkable time we have lived through.

Laughter and tears mingle as teammates and competitors, black and white, coaches and classroom teachers, exchange Tommy stories and embellish one another's stories.

My recorder works full-time, and my eyes gleam as I collect anecdotes, more important now than ever. Earlier I had heard a teenager ask, "Who is this Tommy Jones we're naming our gym for?" And it hurt to know something so real to so many has faded into history. It also brought pride to have been a part of that history.

The new plaque says it briefly, coolly, but it cannot convey all that this person behind the facts generated. Or all that his fellows did with him, because of course he could not have done it alone. Nor can the plaque tell, as one fellow player relates, of a racial slur from the opposing fans, shrugged off by Tommy, who signaled his teammates to do the same.

A time of great social change, indeed.

And so this work is about how one small town handled that transitional time. Today's younger generation, black and white, are a little incredulous as they listen to how things were half a century ago. *Segregation? What's that? Here? In this town? Why did you put up with that?* They don't have a clue. That speaks well, I guess, for our progress. But they need to know their real history, hear firsthand how it was and what we did about it. Right now they don't "have time" to look into it. When they do, we who can tell it will be gone.

So primarily this story is for them, that they might know their heritage of courageous citizenship.

Also, this is for people like us, in other places, who have their own "same kind of different" stories, to let them know how we have grown here and perhaps inspire some of them to exchange and record their own down-home histories before all the tellers are gone. These accounts have never been nor will ever be in the newspapers or textbooks. And they are the truest history.

This printed work was conceived from conversations with some of my former students soon after I retired from teaching. But it was a gleam in the eye long before that, perhaps when as a third grader I was shunned because of my German ancestry. That was the late thirties, and I later learned that Germans throughout the United States faced various prejudicial attitudes because of Hitler's activities in Europe, but the experience gave this eight-year-old child a lifelong empathy for anyone discriminated against for nothing that she had done.

In my first conversations with former students as adults, we revealed some things to one another that surprised and touched us both. I thought then, maybe there are other blacks and whites like us, who don't know one another's hearts, and maybe our stories could awaken them to exchange their treasures of memory.

Then in 1989 a book showing both admiration and scorn for the West Texas obsession with football became a hot topic hereabouts, with its references to racial prejudice in the area, specifically in Crane with its infamous Wall between the Races. Thus was fanned the fire of my obsession with the subject of how this community in the desert southwest navigated the shifting sands of integration and the need to get the real story/stories out.

With the Tommy celebration, we know we must tell about how we were and how we got that way, about how we grew and changed, and mostly about some remarkable people. Perhaps this is a novel, albeit nonfiction, for that's what it was for me as I lived it, some of it vicariously, a real page-turner from the day I arrived here in the fifties. I had to be filled in on the town's first years through real live flashbacks—conversations and interviews with folks who had been here from the beginning.

It is not all about basketball or football or even about sports in general.

It's a drama with a setting and a plot like few others. The setting was a natural happening and instigated the plot. What's memorable here is the characters who showed up to pilot that plot.

It's in the air tonight that everyone here remembers his part in the drama, sensing the significance of the tale we all helped write.

Maybe it's a report, an extensive news story, with much editorializing between the authentic quotations. Every oral word quoted here I heard with my own ears, and 98 percent of those words are recorded and accompanied by a full transcription in the County Historical Commission's Archives. So while I vouch for the authenticity of the quotes, I cannot always vouch for their accuracy. Some reports contradict one another, but isn't that what reporting is? Isn't that life? These people stick by their accounts, whether another agrees or not. And a true reporter gives each a forum for his view.

Neither did I make like an English teacher and turn their informal, even colloquial, language to formal. Personality shines through word choices, stops and starts, even some repetitions.

Whatever, the report is as accurate as we can make it.

And after each chapter is a note page or two for the reader's own additions of fact or opinion.

From *El Ave '66,* CHS yearbook:

"A" BASKETBALL TEAM

DeWayne Ervin, Hayne Hamilton, Lynn Shelton, Gary Gaines, Bob McKay, Glenn Fletcher, Eddie Dee Jones, Billy Van Jones, Mike Waggoner, Tommy Jones, Coach Jack Gothard (front)

From *El Ave '69*

"A" TEAM

FRONT ROW: Louie Jones, David Morgan, Benny Wilson, John Teel, Ronnie Willis, Ronnie Gurley, Tim Atkinson; BACK ROW: Coach Arlen White, Randy Robbins, Billy Owens, Terry Neal, Captain Tommy Jones, Captain Jimmy Burr, Jackie Jeffery, Ricky Anderegg

Tommy's teammates in 2011:
Front: Jackie Jeffery, Coach Arlen White, Randy Robbins, Billy Owen
Back: Clarence Neal, Terry Neal, Ronnie Willis, Ricky Anderegg; Louie Jones, manager, was shown in the 1969 yearbook picture but was behind the camera for this one.

Tommy's wife Pat Jones and Arlen White

Tommy and Pat Jones's daughter and her children

I

THE MOTIVATION

To tell our story about a wall and its demolition, both concrete and abstract, I had to go back to the beginning. I wasn't here at the beginning but came early enough to find many charter settlers who filled me in.

It was six men of Indostan
To learning much inclined,
Who went to see the Elephant
(Though all of them were blind),
That each by observation
Might satisfy his mind.
The First approached the Elephant,
And happening to fall
Against his broad and sturdy side,
At once began to bawl:
"God bless me! But the Elephant
Is very like a WALL!"
★★★
And so these men of Indostan
Disputed loud and long,
Each in his own opinion,
Exceeding stiff and strong,
Though each was partly in the right,
But all of them were wrong.

—John Godfrey Saxe, "The Blind Men and the Elephant"[2]

Chapter 1

OF LIGHTS AND A WALL

EVELYN ROSSLER STRODER

The wall—five feet high and built of concrete and rock and mortar alongside the black/colored/Negro section of Crane—had been in place some four decades when writer H. G. Bissinger walked down the hall in Crane High School where I taught English and journalism. Later, a coach told me Bissinger was spending the school year at Permian High School in Odessa, thirty-plus miles north, to look into and write about the phenomenon that is Texas schoolboy football.

He had made a good selection, I remember thinking, as the Permian Panthers were one of the winningest teams in the state. Their head coach, Gary Gaines, Crane graduate and an old favorite of mine, had come into great acclaim with his team's successes. So it seemed natural for the writer to visit here for background and understanding, as several Permian key players and personnel also had roots in Crane.

His story, some said, would remind us of Hoosiers, a fact-based novel about an Indiana high school basketball team. But when *Friday Night Lights* came out, there was anything but a Hoosier-style reaction.

In the Permian/Odessa community, there was anger because he quoted racial and sometimes foul language used by some assistant coaches (never Gaines). Anger because he described the rearrangement of school districts that "happened" to put some powerful football players in the Permian district, in the newer and "classier" of the two Odessa high schools. Anger because he reported some veiled threats Gaines had received from parents.

The writer was loudly accused of misrepresenting the racist climate, of misquoting school officials, of "just revving things up, trying to make money off us," and the like. But it is significant that there was not one lawsuit or formal charge of any kind.

One parent of a younger person involved in the story said to me, "He just told the truth, didn't he?" As far as I could tell, yes.

In Crane, the folks who were angry—not a majority but a very vocal minority—had a visual focus.

THE WALL THAT FAILED

It was the wall.

What the Writer Saw

Bissinger's view of the originally two-block-long edifice beside Crane's black community had come from L. V. Miles, uncle and guardian of James "Boobie" Miles, outstanding black running back for the Permian Panthers. L.V. himself had grown up in Crane during the forties.

First Bissinger pitched a town that fathers liked because there was "ready work in the oilfield," mothers liked because there were "few temptations that could entice their offspring," and children liked because "they hadn't been anyplace else. It had, for many people, all the comfortable feelings and fixtures of a small town." Then came the fast curve.

> But for L. V. Miles, as for a handful of others who had the same skin color, the Crane he grew up in might as well have been on another planet.
>
> His life had been defined by a five-foot-high wall of rock and concrete. It ran along a street and had been built so the whites who lived around the edge of Niggertown would not have to see it. L.V. and the handful of other blacks who lived in this town of thirty-eight hundred people [in the forties and fifties] could do whatever they wanted inside that wall; no one really cared. But whenever they ventured outside it, it was without welcome.[3]

Thus was shown a believable background for L.V.'s passion to give his nephew a chance the uncle had never had—to play high school football. Nearly any teacher and/or parent can empathize with such a desire, especially for a young man who needed a direction for his life and an outlet for his physical and mental energy.

Bissinger also said the only time L. V. ever had contact with whites was during summer league baseball, but otherwise he stayed behind the concrete wall that "fenced him and his friends in like cattle," and "he wasn't allowed to go to high school football games unless he climbed a light pole or snuck under a fence."[4]

[Fact: by the late fifties, blacks were allowed to attend football games like other people, though they were assigned their own "colored section." I remember being a little self-conscious when I walked past these bleachers with my children and spoke to a few black people I knew from elsewhere, and those folks spoke to us.]

But while the wall was a focus in Crane, it was just a dot in the racist landscape Bissinger portrayed in the area. After he received several threats to his physical safety, Bissinger moved his book-signing engagement from Odessa to Midland. That meant Craneites had to drive about fifty miles instead of thirty to get an autographed copy.

What Locals Saw

What a furor the writer's commentary caused hereabouts. From the DQ to the drugstore, classrooms to churches, letters in the local weekly to feature articles in area daily newspapers, it was a subject to have an opinion on. Some indignant folks said that the concrete structure referred to had been part of a fence around an equipment yard, and everything else was lore. Turns out there was—and is—more lore than documentation. But within that lore are the deepest truths.

With several of my friends and former students, black and white, I already had a dialogue going about segregation/integration, as we had realized that if we didn't set the record straight, later generations would never know what really had happened in the twentieth century here. Now that dialogue turned toward the wall.

I vaguely remembered the structure somewhere in the northwest section of town had something to do with setting off the old colored (a more polite term than *black,* my generation was taught) part of town. But I had thought little of it as I visited friends in the area and ran teacher errands to the former Bethune School for blacks, which building had since the late sixties been the Bethune Annex to the Crane school system.

Material on the subject, for researchers as well as just talkers, developed exponentially. Every newspaper letter or feature brought on new comments, in addition or correction or rebuttal. Every conversation around town sparked another as someone mentioned his or a friend's related experience. My request via an ex-students' school Internet newsletter[5] brought innumerable e-mail responses from former students and teachers, every comment a little different from any other.

What Was/Is It, Really?

It had been a required delineation for an FHA housing addition ... retaliatory action by a disappointed candidate for office ... safeguard to prevent children in the northwest neighborhood from playing on the equipment next door ... boundary of a dairy or a ranch to keep the animals in. And then there was the response, "What wall?" by one black former student who was prominent in Odessa politics.

But while the hearsays, denials, and elaborations were rife, Ellis Lane, who had been among the first wave of black students to attend the integrated Crane High School, and Sue Christon, a graduate of all-white CHS a few years ahead of Ellis, cast the first light of documentation on the subject.

Soon after publication of *Lights,* Sue Neeley Christon visited Lane, then a Crane County commissioner, in his office at the courthouse. She said that her daddy—Leon Neeley, an early Crane developer and promoter—had built that wall. He had loved the black people, she said, and would not have built anything for reasons of hate, and she asked Lane's help in finding the records to prove it. Sue had her own documentation from childhood deep within her, but she wanted something concrete to show, largely to exonerate her daddy from charges of racism. So they looked into the records and found this, as reported by Ellis in a black history program at the county library in the nineties.

What Ellis Found

After World War II, Neeley and others wanted to build FHA-insured houses on several blocks of land in the northwest section of town. That land was part of "tent city" in this town still in its teenage years. The folks living there were mostly black, and they were "squatters," with no utilities, no ownership of land, living in tents and makeshift houses.

When the prospective builders contacted state housing authorities, they found a state/federal requirement that must preclude the building of houses in the new Park Addition. The black population must be moved from the area in or near where the new houses were to be built.

"Also," Ellis said, "the place where the blacks were located had to be clearly separated from the white part of town." Since Crane had no railroad tracks, river, or the like, a wall was built to make that clear separation.

"So it wasn't built out of hate, after all. Just business—greed, maybe, but not hate."

As Ellis made that report, I found a sweet irony in the fact that the Faith in Christ Church (not all black membership) sat—as it still does—on land adjacent to the FHA housing addition and in the exact area that blacks had been moved from a half century earlier—with Ellis as its pastor.

But apart from the FHA approval matter, Sue Christon has no doubt about her personal, on-site knowledge of the wall's origin—or at least part of it.

"This is not hearsay," she said, "as I heard it for myself." It was that familiar phenomenon of life, that children instinctively save in

THE WALL THAT FAILED

memory things they do not understand, save them until they can fit them together with other data for an epiphany of sorts, where meanings come together to illuminate one another.

Sue said after the black population had been relocated, most in their own homes, exactly two blocks west of the planned FHA housing area, and building in the Park Addition was under way, Neeley had sold acreage between the two sections to a roustabout company.

"They had those big trucks with chains hanging down," she said, "and I heard Bill Hollins tell Daddy about spying black children playing on the trucks and other equipment, forbidden though they may have been. Bill said he was afraid the kids would get hurt." Hollins was a black man who was "good friends" with Neeley, according to his son Don, and also according to Sue.

"Daddy said, 'Well, I have some concrete slabs I was about to haul off, so we'll just build a wall along there.'" Neeley, lauded in one newspaper article of his day as a farsighted developer who helped pull Crane up by its bootstraps, often had junk piles of salvaged concrete slabs from cement foundations, sidewalks, and the like.

She recalled four men put up the wall, clearly made of odd-shaped slabs of concrete cemented in a random mosaic pattern. As a clincher to her memory about its purpose, Sue likes to point out that the wall was troweled smooth on the side facing west but rough on the side facing the equipment yard.

Herein lay confusion at first, but the pieces ultimately fit together when we remembered the wall former Bethune students saw was two blocks long. A look at the town plat shows the first block of Negro housing in the area was just southwest of the school, and the FHA-required wall was one block long just east of that tract. Neeley had deeded that area to Bill Hollins, who sold or otherwise transferred individual lots to other blacks.

Here is where Sue's memory fits in. More blacks built—or moved in—homes in the next block south, and many of those houses were/are across the narrow Gloria Street from the equipment yard site.

Official documentation for the federal restriction of separating the races is not hard to find in government records all over the South/Southwest. Neither are "clearly delineated" living places for blacks. Of course, there are no such barriers in "sundown towns," those cities that did not allow a black person to reside in the city at all, or even be there overnight.[6]

Other geographical dividers were used to separate blacks from whites throughout the whole South and much of the North. Crane's wall seems almost unique, but there is at least one other—not in the Deep South or even the West but in Detroit, Michigan.

Sometimes called Detroit's mini-Berlin Wall, sometimes called the Wailing Wall, this seemingly innocent-looking fence has a familiar history but is much more imposing visually than the Crane wall. After World War I, some black residents moved into a then rural and vacant area near the edge of Detroit, and when a developer sought to build homes for middle-income whites nearby, he ran into the same problem Neeley had. To secure FHA loan approvals, the Detroit builder put up a wall six feet high, one foot in width, and one-half mile in length to separate clearly the white and black areas.

This separation as a federal requirement should not be construed as federal prejudice—though such may have existed—as it seems here an economic factor. Whites generally would not buy homes close to blacks, and the Federal Housing Authority could or would not guarantee loans on houses that would be a hard sell or resell.

What Estiene Declared

After Ellis's report, Estiene Bishop, who said she *is* black history in Crane, gave a different take on the reason for the wall.

Speaking at a Mount Zion Church anniversary, she said she knew about Ellis's documentation and thought not much of it.

As with all such quotes, this is presented in Estiene's exact words, with no sanction or denial of her opinions and no modification of her language. Additional facts are inserted by this writer for clarity only.

Something I want y'all to know is about the history of that fence down there. I've heard so much talk about that fence, who done this and who done that, but the first thing I want you to know is the reason why that fence is there.

Not what they say they had in the courthouse—if they got that in the courthouse, they got a lie in the courthouse—but that fence is down there because Leon Neeley, he ran for commissioner. He wanted the black people to vote for him. He carried some of us up there to vote. We didn't vote for him. He didn't get to be commissioner. So he divided the blacks from the whites. He put us over here, and this was going to be Niggertown [sic]. We weren't people no more, because we didn't vote for him.

That's the reason. And I can tell you who built that fence. It was my brother, my oldest brother, Louie Jones, Junior; my sister-in-law's husband (she can witness this), Gus Walker; and Bill Hollins (the one that had the money, because he worked for—he came here to work for—Leon Neeley). He had more money than Neeley, 'cause he *saved his* money, and Neeley spent his.

When it was time to buy the land, Mr. Neeley had to get Bill to buy the land to sell to the black people. So he did that. The men who built that fence were working for Leon Neeley.

And I have witnesses today—the ones who tore down half of that fence are here. You all know them very well: Reverend Jeffery, Sister Jeffery, and the Neal brothers—and there were some more of them. [Here Estiene exchanged knowing smiles with a number of nodding men *and* women in the congregation.]

Sister Neal was telling me, she said, "I was out there in the back watching for them while they tore the fence down." That's why that fence got torn out, as much of it as did. And we'll say—we've been through it here.

[Evidently her reference is to the original one-block-long fence just north of the part still standing. Timing of this next event is not clear, though I have heard several vague references to it. I never questioned Estiene about the date.]

They sent a letter to our pastor, and told him that they wanted all Niggers [sic] out of town, or in three days they would kill them all. But now we—that didn't scare us. We all had our guns, and we were going to sit there and wait. My sister-in-law told me [recently]—"Yeah, but I was in the scaredy bunch. I ran." [Laughter in the congregation.]

And I want you all to know I don't care what nobody tells you. I'm telling you the history, the gospel truth. I'm telling you because I've been here for the last—I ain't going to say how many years. I've been through it all. We've had some good days. We've had some bad days. We've had some of all kind of days, but we're still here.[7]

Myriad Perceptions—All Valid

Beyond these documentable—or virtually so—claims, the fence and its function have negative, iffy, and positive meanings. Ugliness, like beauty, is in the eye of the beholder, and what it has been or is to anyone is what it is, just as surely as if it were on official paper. Some have said Miles's view of the wall was biased. Well, of course. Who ever heard of such a many-faceted symbol's having *unslanted* views? This can't be pictured in a comprehensive aerial photo; it's down-on-the-ground meaningful, depending on where one stands on that ground. What L.V. Miles said it was, it *was* to him. Not how someone else's life was defined, but how L.V.'s was.

It's reminiscent of John Godfrey Saxe's poem, "The Blind Men and the Elephant," which retells an ancient parable illustrating human nature regarding perspectives. Each man "saw" the elephant from his own position. But regarding the Crane wall, we must reverse Saxe's conclusion and say, "While each of them was partly in the wrong, all of them were right." In a Jain (Indian religion that emphasizes nonviolence) version of the story, the king tells the blind men, "All of you are right ... every one is telling it differently because each ... touched the different part of the elephant. So actually the elephant has all the features you mentioned."[8]

Thus it is with each person who sees the wall. Though each may be partly in the wrong, each is right as to what it is to him/her.

Younger Folks Remember

Still another view of the wall's purpose was remembered to me by Alice Burns Lowery, CHS grad in the fifties. She visited quite often with the Brown girls, in their home beside the equipment yard managed by their father Horace Brown, for the J. Cleo Thompson Oil Company.

"The stone wall ran on one side of the yard and the Brown home," Alice said, "and I always understood it was there to help fence the equipment in." Many of the Browns' friends had thought the same thing, and I see it as a credit to the Brown family and their associates that it seems never to have become a talking topic.

Then I heard from Jannye Brown Wimberley, one of three girls in the family, about her "unobstructed view of the wall" and how as a girl she had learned its function.

> My family came to Crane in June 1952, at the end of
> my sixth-grade year, and lived in the house owned
> by J. Cleo Thompson at the corner of Katherine and

Second Streets, and I lived there until I married in 1958. [My dad worked for Mr. Thompson.]

We had moved from a very small town about seventy-five miles northwest of Fort Worth, a town of about five hundred people that had an awful rule that no one of African American descent could be in town after dark on penalty of death. This is shameful but it happened. [Black] people could not get anything to eat—only get gas and leave as quickly as possible.[9]

So when she and her family moved from that "sundown town" to Crane, at first Jannye thought it was "nice" that this town let African Americans live here. Then she learned what the wall meant.

> I was walking on the wall in back of my house, and I said hi to a little boy playing [on the other side]. His mother immediately came out and told him to go in the house. I told her he was fine, but she looked at me and asked, "Are you trying to get him killed?"
>
> I said no one would hurt him, and she informed me that he could get hurt just for talking to me, so for me to leave him alone. I said I was sorry, that that was the last thing I would ever want.
>
> This was within the first few weeks of our moving there. I could not believe it, but I was careful never to put another child in that kind of danger.
>
> [Several years later] my parents were across the street visiting, and I had gone into their bedroom and turned on the light when a man outside the window said something to me. Needless to say, I was scared half to death. My sister called our parents, who rushed home and called the police. When the police came and asked for a description, I told him the man was white, with curly blond hair, and about the same height as my dad, I thought.

Even after this description, police asked her several times whether she was sure he was not black, until Jannye told them rather vehemently that she "did know the difference between white and black!"

Daisy Lane Jeffery, grad from the sixties and now a CHS teacher, was nearly a generation after Jannye, and when I asked her a while back, "So, you all didn't think of living, or just wandering, outside that wall?" Daisy's response was a gentle but increasingly emphatic, "Oh, no ... no, No, NO!"

When I later asked Daisy to elaborate her views of the wall, she said merely that she relies on the people who lived there at the time and what they say.

Then Louie Jones, who is black and a few years behind Daisy, knew what it was supposed to mean but had never felt very intimidated by it.

"That's just the way things were. I knew all that, but I don't think it stopped me. I think it was there to hold us back psychologically, and physically, and every other way, but I don't think it did."

Only Tricks

Louie's generation (he graduated in 1971) would regularly, every Halloween, work at tearing down the wall.

"In a way, we had already knocked it down," Louie said, "because we were at that time going to school with the white people, but physically it was still there. We would take chunks of it out every year, and I don't know why we chose Halloween, but that was what we did every year. We just left it there. No one approached us or said anything at all about it."

Ellis Lane, a high school senior the year we integrated, said he helped finish off the north half of the wall on—yes—Halloween night.

He said he had never paid any attention to it until then. Still, Ellis thinks of the wall and the community behind it as safety and security.

"It was a place of protection for us," he said, and told of a kind of "sundown community" in reverse. "We [kids] didn't want any white people there after dark, and if they stayed, we'd rock 'em." I couldn't help thinking his parents would have put a stop to the "rocking," had they known about it.

Some Anglo students too have told of helping to tear down the wall.

So that was the trend among the younger generations as soon as they were aware of the structure's function: tear it down. And that is how our marker came to be.

Tear the Thing Down

A civic-minded but relatively new resident had read my column on the subject in the local newspaper and called to ask me whether the wall was real. Then he made a well-intended suggestion but one that made me shiver.

"Some of us ought to get together and tear that thing down."

Oh, no, I thought. That's what they do in places like Tiananmen Square, Beijing, China—eradicate every evidence of something undesirable to the effect that one day some could/would say, oh, that never really happened.

No, Mark It

Our Historical Commission was already into the Oral History Project when I mentioned what I had heard about tearing down the remaining part of the wall, and the idea of marking it as a part of our history took off immediately. Most of us had already heard folks denying the wall's function, and we feared some future generations might deny its existence.

Because getting a Texas historical marker, if approved, would take a year or so, the consensus was that this was urgent enough for us to do it ourselves and have it ready for presentation a few months later at the all-school reunion.

The project, chaired by Debby McFarland Cowden, former editor of the Crane High School student newspaper, took untold hours of planning and implementing those plans. History teacher Raymond Ifera and former student and later art teacher Lou Young, both also professional artists, volunteered their time and connections to give us the best deal on having a plaque cast for the wall, as well as one for the original all-black Bethune School building.

Countless others gave their input, as Ms. Very Thorough Debby called frequent meetings of commission members and anyone else interested at every stage of the planning. Payment for the wording on the plaque was by the letter, so that had to be concise to be economical. But when the dedication of the markers became a celebration of unity, all I heard from agreed it had been so worthwhile. The festival of love and appreciation and forgiveness vindicated what some had long felt: Craneites of many colors already cared for one another as individuals, and now our open dialogue was sure to help with the collective racism.

Brother Bowens, Little Miracle for Our Time

As we began to gather near the time for the ceremonies, apprehension and suspense were palpable, as there was some doubt whether our key speaker would be there. He was Rev. H. A. Bowens, longtime pastor of the Mount Zion Church, now retired, and just a few days earlier he had been driving alone and become disoriented. Someone called his home for family members to come to another town to get him and his car.

So there was suspense that morning, as some wondered who might fill in as speaker at the school. Or whether the speaker at the wall marker would mind speaking twice. But to our delight, just before program time, Rev. Bowens and his wife, Bucilla Abron Bowens, appeared at the Bethune School, both looking fresh as daisies with nary a hint of having been sick. And there was no confusion or disorientation in his message about bringing up a child in the way he should go and trusting the Holy Spirit to take over when the child had outgrown parental discipline.

Mrs. Bowens had reared most of her children as a single mother and then married the widower Rev. Bowens a few years earlier. She and others agreed her husband's recovery for this time was providential.

Many were the memories shared that day—some surprising, some expected. Bowens, who after his retirement from pastoring at Mount Zion Church then served as pastor at Faith Baptist Church in Kermit, was introduced by Cowden, chairman of the Marker Committee for the Historical Commission.

What a delight it was to record for our museum and our posterity this casual, conversational talk, calmly presented and interspersed with humor and yet with such an easy-to-follow theme.

His first remark brought considerable laughter. But I believe nearly everyone there knew that, while he can talk a long time about love for his God and his fellow man, he is also wise enough to get to the point concisely when necessary. And they listened.

> Now I have my full-sized Bible here, and it is going to at least take me two or three hours for what I have to say.
>
> But seriously, I am glad to be asked to speak a few words about this school and the black community in Crane.
>
> I came here in 1950, and it was an unusual town. All of the people were very friendly. Ed Mayes was willing to house me, and the first couple of months were free. We only had about three telephones in the area, and if anyone got a call, a neighbor would run you down so that you wouldn't miss it. It was a nice place.

THE WALL THAT FAILED

The houses were kinda run down, but there were a lot of children. They did a lot of racing in the streets. And they would be racing, and all of a sudden they would stop and do like this. [Brushing his legs, feet.] It was them goatheads.

They learned to respect those goatheads.[10]

We had a preacher back then, by the name of T. J. Hollins. Brother Hollins had a following. All of the houses were his, and all of the children were the same—they were his children. You just couldn't take one of his services [lightly or disrespectfully].

And all the children would show respect in church, because if they didn't, Brother Hollins might come down from the pulpit and bop a head or two. If he would do this to this certain child, I had the notion that he would do it to mine, and so I urged respect. These children would fear and respect what was behind that [discipline], and that's a good thing. We all need discipline until we learn that—you're not goin' to do that—about certain things.

And while they were learning it this way, the Holy Spirit on the inside was telling them what was right.

On Tuesdays, Mrs. Amanda Lane would see to it that all the children would come to Junior Church. And that within itself created an atmosphere protected by love because the Bible plainly tells us that the fear of the Lord is the beginning of wisdom.

And the boys that participated in basketball under Professor Hall learned respect.

Professor Hall evidently was a God-fearing man, and he was a great teacher. He planted something in those boys that showed: sometimes Professor Hall would be away from them when they were practicing or playing, and yet the boys still abided by his rules.

If you bring me up right, if you give me the training that you ought to give me, after I'm old enough, and get out in this rough world, that will come up, and teach me how to walk, how to respect my fellow man, and how to reverence my God. That attitude I saw in Crane has helped me, as I pastored here for some twenty-six years.

Before I began the ministry here, Herbert Christian, pastor of the First Baptist Church, said we ought to build a better house of the Lord for the Mount Zion congregation. And we of both congregations did put our labor together and do that. Bless his heart.

A Legacy Holds

Brother Bowens returned to his main theme just before closing:

The legacy we leave behind is to train a child in the way he should go. Now I'm not saying all of them will stay the way, but a whole lot of them will. I was talking to my baby boy a few days ago, George Bowens—he has been one of the professors in the Abilene school system for twenty-eight years—and he agrees that his training has come back all along.

But what I'm trying to say is that if you do your job, when the children outgrow the head-bopping, and you are not there to say, "Don't do that," the Holy Spirit will take your place. Right? Yes, he will.

The Spirit of the Lord is the beginning of wisdom, and you all know that.

That's all I've got to say. Thank you.

And many thanked Pastor Bowens for those words.

After this, Debby opened the forum for others, and several responded joyfully, sentimentally, and emotionally.

Bill Estes, former tennis coach and longtime middle school principal, seemed eager to speak first.

> If you want to have an experience, come over here some evening about sundown, in the wintertime, and I'm sure you're going to hear the refrains of "Sweet Georgia Brown" coming out of this gym, and Elmo Morris is going to be walking up and down. He was the designated motivator.
>
> I'll tell you one thing, when the schools from other towns came in here and got off the bus, they knew they were in for a fight. If you came for a game, those Leopards were going to get after you. From the time you got here, they were going to thrash you until the time you left.
>
> And you could go in this building and you could go to that home economics window, and get you some catfish and onions for thirty-five or fifty cents, and you'd go in that gym, and this event—it was an event—belonged to the black community. It's about the only thing we allowed them to have. [His voice broke at this point, but he recovered with a smile to continue.]
>
> I thank God for the memories I have from when Bill Teague, Gordon Morgan, and others of us got to work the ball games down here and share in this unique experience. And I know that if you come by here some evening you'll hear the chants of, "We want a hundred! We want a hundred!"

Scoreboard Fun Remembered

He was referring to an example of how the community could take something others might call an annoyance and turn it into a focus for inspiration and fun. The aged scoreboard showed only two digits, so when the score approached the upper nineties, enthusiasm as reckoned by the noise became palpable, and when the board rolled over to double zeros, deafening was a mild word for the sound waves in that gym.

Patty Webb, CHS grad who had also been on the local school board, the first woman elected after a judicial ruling that forbade their exclusion, asked to speak.

> I was always down here, with my dad. I never knew there was a "wall," because I was always here, often at the Dew-Drop Inn with my dad. I called Little Louie's dad my uncle.
>
> My brother Ben and I were walking one day—this is a true story—and a whole bunch of friends were with us, and Ben said, "Oh, there's Uncle Louie. Let's get a ride with him." Uncle Louie drove up and someone said, "This is your uncle?" We crawled in the pickup and said to those other kids, "Y'all wanta ride with us?" They said, "Naw, we better not."
>
> That's what we called him—Uncle Louie.
>
> And when they started going to school with us, I had my blue jeep, and I came down here, and they loaded up, and we went to school together. They're always part of my family.

Annette Lopez Lane began eagerly.

> I started the first grade in Crane, and my daddy, Juan Lopez, and Pink Morris [who was black] took me to school. Other kids made fun of me, but I never paid

any attention. I didn't care. It was fun. But when I was about twelve, I told my daddy I didn't want them to take me to school anymore. Pink said, "Is it because of me?" and I said, "No, it's because the boys see me get out of a truck." That's my memory. It was a long time ago.

Jackie Jeffery, who had attended the Bethune School until 1965, then graduated from CHS and is now pastor of Mount Zion Church, was next.

"I think this is a great experience. To be recognized in unity is a great thing. But it really happened in '65. We had all those accomplishments at the Black school, and then when we integrated—myself, Clarence Neal, and all of us—the winning tradition went on. Tommy Jones was a great player, and I had the privilege of playing with Tommy, and we were—just awesome."

Ellis Lane, Bethune student until his senior year at CHS, said, "We have some great memories, and the clashing that we did was a great thing, because when we got on the court and the football field, we were one. We had to struggle to get there, and from the struggle we have doctors, lawyers, preachers, teachers."

Louie Jones had been collecting names of everyone present, reminding them what a momentous occasion this was. Regardless of what he says here, he had been a first-class journalism student/sports editor, and though he had held many high school and college positions, his first love was still reporting.

"Mrs. Stroder gave me an assignment. You know, she was my teacher, and she's still giving me assignments. I guess I didn't do well enough in school. But I'm supposed to get everybody's names. And those people that I didn't see, please see me before we leave."

Debby was eager to give credit where credit is due.

"And we thank a member of the class of '66, Lou Young, now from Louisiana," she said. "And Ray Ifera—not a Crane graduate but a darn good teacher—and his wife, Sharon, who all saved us from having to pay retail for the plaques. They worked with us, and we appreciate all of their input, their efforts, their expertise because of their line of business. We couldn't have done it without them."

Cookie Lane, who shows her loyalty to today's whole student body, explained her Bethune background.

> I graduated right here, and the reason why you have these championships is we couldn't come home and say we won second. Our parents wouldn't accept that.
>
> This is the honest-to-God truth. They didn't accept no second, no third. If you didn't say first, and your parents were in there watching you, when you got home you got a whupping. They were going to know exactly why you weren't paying attention.
>
> So this is very special to me. We have a lot of guys that's gone now that I really wish could have been here, along with Mr. Hall. But I will accept it [the marker] for our generation.

Billy Pat Butler, earlier CHS grad, said his dad, Pat Butler, had brought him to the basketball games.

> Those guys were awesome, but one thing I remember was about a person Coach Estes brought up—Elmo Morris.
>
> When the Leopards would be getting behind, wouldn't be doing what they should be doing, Elmo would jump up and grab that cigar, and he'd say, "Okay, girls, okay, girls." And there was thunder, because they'd start stomping their feet, and they'd start singing, "Poison Letters." And the girls had a lot to do with those teams. It wasn't just the guys.
>
> But Elmo was known to take a drink.

That last comment, with an affectionate smile and without apology, brought chuckles.

Following these comments, Louie called all Bethune graduates together to sing the school song, which is printed on the plaque. Suffice it to say that, like all school songs I know of, just the words in print don't seem to say much—but when sung by the right people, take on character, emotion, and symbolism beyond the words, almost beyond any words. The song is on the oral history recording available in the museum, but I urge readers to get three or four former Bethune students to sing it for you. Then you'll get it.

After this part of the dedication program at Bethune, the group of about seventy moved a couple of blocks south to the marker at a portion of the old Wall between the Races.

Necessary Comments

Debby Cowden began "to say a few things" before Ellis's talk.

> I wanted to give credit to Mrs. Evelyn Stroder. This was her idea, and through the Crane County Historical Commission a committee was formed. It included Heather Basurto, Jackie Jeffery, Cookie, myself, three commissioners [Mickie Hurst, Louis Overton, and Dennis Young], and Bud Taylor, president of the Crane County Historical Commission. We had lots of support from the city of Crane.

Ellis led in prayer of thanks for "this most blessed day—a day that our Lord has made. We can rejoice and be glad in it." He prayed for blessings on the reunion and all its participants, and gave thanks for all that had happened.

Several amens were heard in the background here, but when Ellis promised that his message would not be long, chuckles were audible. He grinned and went on to thank all who had worked on the dedication project.

On the behalf of the black community, I give thanks to the Historical Commission and the Plaque Committee. We do appreciate it.

["That's right" came from several among the listeners. Ellis continued, and applause and many a "Thank you" came from his listeners as he talked.]

There has been so much controversy, mixed emotion, ill feeling, about this pile of rocks coupled together forming a physical landmark to separate what was called in that day "colored" from the whites. This wall has no barrier on us today, but rather it gives us a growing admiration for our forefathers who lived behind this wall. I didn't understand then, but I understand now, it was their faith in Jesus Christ making them humble enough to subdue this wall.

This is not the only landmark for us to look back and remember, but our landmark is in the hearts of those men and women such as Bill Hollins, Elmo Morris, Jack Lane, Gus Walker, Rev. H. A. Bowens, Louie Jones, Spencer Morris, Duffy Neal, Ed Mayes, Rev. T. J. Hollins, Don Bishop, Louie Jones, Mr. Ernest Hollins, Willie Lee Jeffery, Richard Jeffery, Clifton Thomas, Pink Hollins, Argie Hollins, Walter Jeffery, and many others. Whether facing a railroad track, river bottom, or—yes, even a wall—with humility they did what they could. They didn't give up.

Every wall has to have two sides. That is, in the eyes of God. The wall was just as damaging on one side as it was on the other side. We're here to dedicate this wall. To whom? Our forefathers, they say, "We don't want it." The black generation today says, "We don't want it." The white generation says, "We don't want it." Well, how to dedicate this segregating wall? We the citizens of Crane offer this wall to God, through our Lord and Savior Jesus Christ, who [can] take away the hatred or the reproach that hobbles one's heart.

Today we thank each of you and God for including our forefathers into the vital fibers that are intertwined in the history of Crane. And as a personal note, I thank the Plaque Committee for the opportunity to speak to such a most historical dedication.

But we do have this wall. For its dedication, and on behalf of the black community of Crane, I give thanks to the Historical Commission and the Plaque Committee. A special thanks goes to Evelyn Stroder, Heather Basurto, and others, to let them know, on the behalf of the community, that we do appreciate it. ["That's right" in the background.] We appreciate the untiring dedication and commitment to make this possible. I am standing here in honor of the black forefathers of Crane, who in time constructed this wall.

After Ellis's talk, Charles Stroder, retired Crane high school/middle school math/science teacher, was the first to respond to the invitation to add comments.

"I heard the comments about my wife, which I appreciate, as I know they're true. She presented a paper to the Permian Historical Society about the wall, and if you haven't read that paper, I wish you'd do so. One comment in that paper was that this is a symbol of how far we've come and how far we have to go. And I think that's true."

Here I must confess to a little apprehension when Jo Ann Davenport (now Littleton) asked to speak. Having known Jo Ann in school, I was aware of her tendency to say what she thinks—exactly. I've always appreciated the "what you see is what you get" quality in people, but sometimes it can bring problems with authorities or other hearers. I needn't have worried.

> First let me give praises and honor and thanks to God and to Reverend Bowens, Reverend Lane, Reverend Jeffery, and each of you here. I couldn't stand over there and not say what's on my heart. I thank God for Ed Mayes, who was my great-grandfather, Don Bishop, who was my grandfather, C.J. Drones, my father, all of my extended family, my relatives, and all the citizens of Crane. I'm a firm believer that if you don't acknowledge where you've been, you don't know where you're going. And one of the worst things you can ever do is forget about where you're from. You know, we don't all know where we're going. But our history follows us. Crane was the format, Crane was the stepping stone, for me.
> We all know about *Friday Night Lights*. We all know about the book, we all know about the movie. After the release of the book and then the movie, I was contacted many times by *Time* and *Newsweek* magazines. And each time they would call me and say, "You were on the city council in Odessa during the time of *Friday Night Lights,* and we understand you're from a little town thirty-two miles south of Odessa, and we understand that there's a wall in that community. And we know that racism is running rampant in that community and in Odessa. Can you please share some of the things that happened to you growing up?"
> And it made me upset. First of all, I said, "The wall? What wall? Be more specific." And they would say, "We don't know, but we were told that there's a wall to keep the blacks from the whites." I said, "You know, my parents raised me up to respect and

> honor all people—look at their character, look at their hearts, not the color of their skin." And—you know reporters, Mrs. Stroder, you know how they press you to say negative things so that they can be published—I said, "I grew up in a town where there were seventy-six people in my graduating class, and only four of us were black. So I don't know black, white, and brown."
>
> I could tell you that the issue I have with racism is when I go into a room, and I see all black people, and there's not coalition of people. I have a problem with that. I have to say, "We are all black here. What happened to the brown people? What happened to the white people?" When I walk into a room and I see a rainbow of people, I feel right at home. I love that setting. And if I had not grown up in Crane, that never would have happened, so I thank God for the residents of Crane and my family for my upbringing. [Many an "amen" and "Thank you" and "Bless you."]

Oh, and Jo Ann's take on our racism never made the news magazines. Go figure.

Next, Daisy Lane Jeffery, CHS grad and then a teacher in CHS, said she felt very brave to speak to a crowd not of schoolchildren.

> I'm going to be very brief, but I must say something positive about the community of Crane. My parents' house burned four or five years ago, and the outpouring of love and care and consideration from all people here was just overwhelming. And if anybody ever approached me about racism in Crane, I would have to bring up what I know in my heart, about the people of Crane—very loving and very caring. I guess that happened for such a time as this, because what we experienced through that situation

was just beautiful. So I want to thank all the people of Crane. You are loving, and you are kind.

Again Debby asked whether anyone else wanted to speak before Brother Jackie Jeffery closed the event in prayer. One more time, Louie reminded everyone:

> I need all your names. Because fifty years from now somebody's going to read your name, and they'll know you were here for this historic occasion. [Someone chimed in to say, "His teacher's going to give him an F if he doesn't get them all."]
> But really, if there's anybody I didn't get down at the school, let me get your name now. Mr. Young said that he's always been near the last in any list. He said he'd appreciate if we could move him up a little. So we'll try to do that. [Louie's list is in the end of our story, where Lou's request is honored.]

When Debby asked me to speak, I tried to condense the thoughts swirling inside:

> I think Charles said the main thing that I wanted said, that the wall should be a reminder of how far we still have to go, but I want to mention something else, if I can keep it short, that was in my paper. (That's why I like to write more than speak. When I speak, I use way too many words, and when I write, I can trim it down and make it fit the space and time I have.) But I want to say here that I have never known more gracious people, while and after they have been wronged, than the black people in Crane.
> I have known other people who have been wronged and have been gracious about it afterward, but *all* of my black friends in Crane—I am constantly

astonished, and I really was early on—not only do not act bitter because it took us so long to allow them their God-given rights as Americans, but they graciously express appreciation now that we are finally trying to do what is right. And I would not take anything in the world for being here now. This is truly an historic day, more than most of us may realize right now, and I thank all of you for it.[11]

Media Take Note

Our markers have drawn various media attention, and a remarkable thing to me is the cluelessness of the younger generations. An area newspaper reporter doing a feature for Martin Luther King Day seemed astonished when I said that Crane just happened to have no river or railroad track or the like, but the wall *effect* was common throughout Texas and the South.

"There were barriers like that everywhere?" he asked sharply. Of course, of course, ask your parents and grandparents, I wanted to say to him and others who ask, "Why did you do that?" Likewise, I am told by black friends that their children ask, "Why did you put up with that?"

Impossible to answer except to say that as children we didn't understand but mostly did as we were told—blacks and whites—to stay out of trouble with the system. Then as adults we largely knew that it wasn't right but didn't know how—or didn't have the backbone—to do anything about it. Today, though, some of us have come to value dialogue between the races. How rewarding it has been to talk with former students without the old imposed protocol of society to prevent our speaking from the heart.

Then there was the television interview when an area reporter came to Crane for a feature on the wall just before Martin Luther King Day in 2009.

She met with several people, including black former student Don Hollins, at the site of the marker. The interview was filmed with the deserted equipment yard in the background, alongside a part of the wall that didn't hide the mostly small but neat houses behind it. We were all wearing jackets against the cool, gray day.

Newscaster Jacqueline Sit spoke of Martin Luther King's dream to break down the barriers of segregation, to break down walls just like the one in Crane, to bring communities together.

"It ran for a quarter mile along Gloria Street," she said. "All that's left behind now are remnants that used to divide the black and white communities of the 1940s until integration. Former Crane teacher Evelyn Stroder says it was built to get government housing loans."

Because conversation reveals something extra about the speaker's attitudes, I give a partial transcript of the rest of the interview:

Sit: When segregation was still alive, many parts of the country divided the communities by train tracks or natural barriers such as a river, but since Crane had neither, they built this wall. Some black residents like Don Hollins, who grew up here, reminisce of happy times, saying this divider never even crossed his mind.

Hollins: We would just walk around it, so we just looked at it as a fence, being as we had free access to the town, whenever we wanted to go. The blacks and whites got along.

Sit: In 1965, integration set in. Over the years there have been attempts to get the wall taken down, but advocates say the history needs to be preserved, and so the marker to remember this remains.

Ray Ifera (social studies teacher): Even the negative parts of history need to be preserved. You may just tear down the signs of crematoriums and extermination camps, but you leave something there, you know, as a reminder of what it used to be.

THE WALL THAT FAILED

Sit: Most of the wall has been broken down, [with the remaining part] becoming a symbol of a struggle for a community free of color lines.

Hollins: The wall was just a symbol for the government, and it didn't make a big difference to us. Some [white] people I've been knowing forty-five years; we're friends, and that's that, you know, so this is all good.

Here it seems good to mention that Don's father was Bill Hollins, a black man Sue Christon says was "like a brother" to her father.

That's why some of us "newcomers" who arrived in the fifties and later have learned to listen to those who can enlighten us about the different ways we were and how we got that way.

Location of first wall, looking north toward Bethune School. This is the part students of 70s remember pushing over, approximately where the wire fence stands now.

Second block of wall, looking north toward location of first block, as it stood before marker

Rev. H. A. and wife Bucilla Abron Bowens, just before dedication of Bethune marker

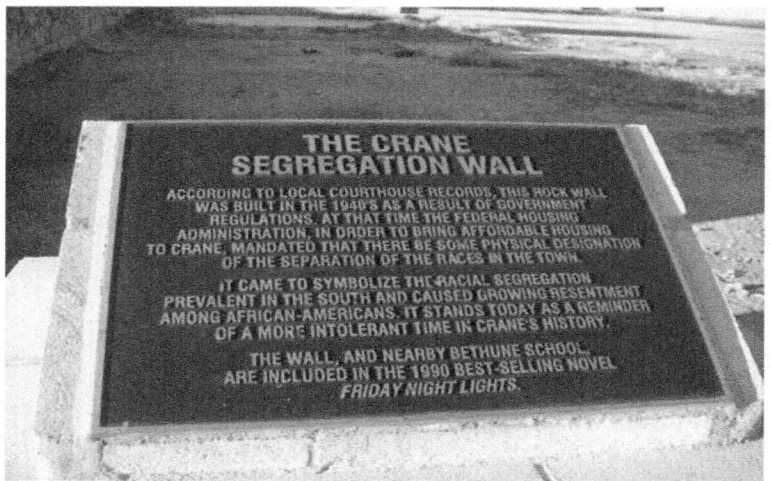

Group of perhaps fifty listening to Ellis's talk at wall marker (Photo by Louie Jones)

Taking pictures of marker as it stood day of dedication (Photo by Louie Jones)

Marker as closed in, tin building removed (Photo by Louie Jones)

Three ministers: Ellis Lane, H. A. Bowens, Jackie Jeffery (Photo by Louie Jones)

After World War I, some black residents of Detroit moved into a then rural and vacant area near the intersection of Wyoming and Eight Mile [streets]. In 1940 a developer sought to build homes for middle income whites in a nearby area. However, the Federal Housing Administration's policies of that era precluded their approving loans in racially mixed areas. To secure FHA approval, this developer put up a wall six feet high, one foot in width and one-half mile in length to clearly separate the white and black areas. His wall led FHA to approve loans for his project.[12]

2 John Godfrey Saxe, "The Blind Men and the Elephant," Wikipedia contributors, "John Godfrey Saxe II," *Wikipedia, The Free Encyclopedia,* https://en.wikipedia.org/w/index.php?title=John_Godfrey_Saxe_II&oldid=718855858 (accessed May 12, 2016).
3 Ibid., 59.
4 H. G.Bissinger, *Friday Night Lights*, 59.
5 Purple and Gold Nuggets is an informal Crane ex-students' newsletter edited by Fredda Arney. It was begun by Jeff Hendderson in the sixties
6 James Loehen, *Sundown Towns: A Hidden Dimension of American Racism* (New York: New Press, 2005).
7 Estiene Bishop, "Church History," speech, Mount Zion Church Anniversary celebration, Crane, Texas, February 8, 2004.
8 John Godfrey Saxe, "The Blind Men and the Elephant," Wikipedia, https://en.wikipedia.org/w/index.php?title=John_Godfrey_Saxe_II&oldid=718855858 (accessed May 12, 2016).
9 Jannye Brown Wimberley, "The Crane Wall," in *Come All Ye Cranes, Do You Recall ...* by Susie Hudson Marines. Omaha, Nebraska: self published, 2012, pp. 201–2.
10 Goathead is a weed common in West Texas. The seed has two little prongs that do give it the appearance of a goat. This "sticker" is a bane to children and others walking through the weeds.
11 Evelyn Stroder, author of *TWTF*
12 Wikipedia contributors, "Detroit Wall," Wikipedia, accessed March 31, 2016, https://en.wikipedia.org/w/index.php?title=Detroit_Wall&oldid=712075000.

READER'S NOTES

II

THE SETTING AND THE CHARACTERS

Time, place, and conditions drew in the people of a certain kind. They were hardy American melting-pot stock, with a touch of the pioneer in their blood, enough tradition to anchor themselves into a community, but also enough pragmatism and humanity to adapt those traditions and customs to their own times.

"Camp kid." There's a magic in those words that only a camp kid understands. A camp kid had a family wherever she roamed ... Everyone took care of everyone.

—Karen Howard Keith[13]

Chapter 2

THE WAYS WE WERE— TOWN KIDS AND CAMP KIDS

Before oil, there was no Crane. The few residents of the county did their official business through Ector County until a town/county seat was established in 1927.

When my husband and I came to Crane in the fifties, it was the beginning of a totally new life—an adventure, no less—for me. Charles had grown up in Wink, another oil field town, but I knew nothing of small towns and even less of the oil field, had never experienced those dust storms that look like a red-brown wall approaching, never gone to the post office for my mail or charged groceries and drugstore items, never felt the intense interest of a whole town in new teachers. But one fact of life was the same here as every other place I knew of.

Segregation was as usual, Texas style, nothing to be noticed or remarked on. It was like other places I'd known—if colored people lived there at all, they had their own section of town.

We knew only that this was one of the highest-paying school districts in Texas, where openings for new teachers were rare, and that my husband had been very lucky to find a job here. He had come to Corpus Christi as a geologist with a major oil company, and that's what he was doing when we married. But various other circumstances in our lives had led him to try teaching as a career—and he liked it. I was very pregnant and would not be teaching for a while, so this was a chance to leave the minimum-pay schools of South Texas.

This only child of Crane County, sired by the oil boom, was barely a teenager when WWII began. It was populated largely by folks from East Texas and points farther east, hardworking folks who brought with them their work ethic, their appreciation for a good job—and their southern customs/unwritten laws.

What Brought Us Here—Migration with Age-Old Purpose

Most who came west were jaded farmers who needed work with real pay, young proven workers who wanted to keep their jobs, and wildcatters hoping for riches from the ground. Then came builders, merchants, doctors, druggists, educators, and others needed to make a real town. This included black people who also came for the job, for better pay than they had known eastward.

The new inhabitants—all of them—pragmatically shaped the town for themselves, keeping their old customs and way of life as they wished, modifying as they required for the life they were building. It was a boomtown. It was an adventure. It was bustling and busy, casual and laid back, all at the same time.

But it was not simply a transplanted eastern town. There was no local tradition, no historic family heritage, no "establishment" or upper class in charge. No one lived in the old home place— except a handful of ranching families only a generation or so older than the town, living around the county. Adventure was not the motive for bankrupted farmers and the like trying to come out of the Depression. New Deal be darned, it still didn't put bread on the table for folks like Sam Stroder, my father-in-law.

Many a man like him was more than happy to come to the oil field for even a day-to-day job of manual labor, for a real paycheck that didn't depend on the weather or the market. And day labor held the hope of going to work full-time for one of the big-name companies or independent operators who had struck it lucky just in time for the market that would intensify with the coming of WWII. I have heard it said many times of those days that if you got on with a major company and "made 'em a hand," you were set for life. This was for whites, of course. Sam Stroder hunted such a job after first tentative ventures into the oil country.

In my husband's just-for-family autobiography, he wrote about those times.

> Several times while we lived on the farm in Navarro County, during the slack farming times, my dad would go out to the west Texas oil fields to find temporary work.
>
> Sometimes he would travel by bus or train, but at times he would have to "ride the rails," travel as a hobo sneaking rides in boxcars.
>
> Every freight train had many, many such men "down on their luck," and it was no disgrace but

rather honorable to make such a sacrifice to provide for their families. In later years I remember Daddy's pointing to some depot loading dock and remarking that he had slept there. He also said that he had never begged for food, but always had something to eat.

He would usually find some work (hard and low-paying) and bring me a present. One time he brought me a dollar watch, and no one who ever owned a Rolex was any prouder than I was of that watch.

The Long-Awaited Reprieve

In September of 1935, we were in the field picking cotton, and Aunt Lola drove up with a telegram from brother-in-law Carey Hawkins saying that he had a fairly steady job for Daddy at Lee's Store, Texas, "but to hurry." Daddy left his cotton field that day and went to the oil field. He told the Negro working for him to take the crop. Mother and I stayed in Navarro until November, when we joined him.

We rode the train to Big Spring and ate food from box lunches that the porter sold. No dining cars for the Stroders.

I remember how lost I felt when we got to Big Spring. The Suttles Hotel looked like a skyscraper to me. But we were with my Dad and had a new life ahead. I am sure my parents were a little apprehensive, but they never let me see it.

In later years some historians have called those days the "Last Great Westward Migration." Hundreds or maybe thousands left small, worn-out farms in the east for the West Texas oil fields. Boom towns such as McCamey (1920), Wink (1926), Crane (1927), and Iraan (1928), had sprung up next to the newly discovered oil fields. Small, already-established towns such as Andrews, Kermit, and Odessa now grew rapidly due to the oil activity.

The jobs were many but seldom quite enough to go around, so always at a premium. I have heard Sam say that at first the hours were longer than the paycheck was for, but it you didn't like that, you could "hit the road," as there was always a line of folks wanting your job.

The Offer That Couldn't Be Refused

Keeping an already good job was what brought the Weisers west.

Mary Ruth Speight Weiser turned twenty years old on Pearl Harbor Day, 1941. Except for the darkness of war shadowing her country, life had a happy outlook. She and her husband, Denzel, were expecting their first child the next spring, and Denzel had a job with a major oil company—which usually meant lifetime security.

About the second week in December, Denzel and several of his coworkers were pulled from their offshore jobs in Louisiana to await reassignment. Nice timing—now the young couple could be free for Christmas with family in the little town where they both had both grown up. A poignant little essay, "The Long Road Ahead," from her scrapbook tells what happened next:

> We planned to spend Christmas in
> Hankamer, Texas. The tree was at
> Mother's (Hallie Ruth), the dinner
> with Dad and Mama (Weiser).
> We had just moved from Buras, La.,
> as the Gulf Oil Company had shut down
> some of their operations, and we
> did not expect to be called before
> the new year.

> About a week before Christmas the
> Gulf Office called and said we were
> transferred to West Texas, and were
> to report immediately.
>
> We packed, hurriedly opened our
> Christmas gifts, and headed West.
> We arrived in Crane on December 22, 1941.

From Hankamer, they drove five hours one afternoon to spend the night with an aunt, and the next day they "made pretty good time," she wrote her mother, "arriving here in Odessa in about eight hours." As Mary Ruth was writing that letter, Denzel came in to say they were being sent to Crane, some thirty miles south.

"It is a pretty nice place, from what they say," she wrote.

But they went to Crane that afternoon, and the next day they drove around to look unsuccessfully for a better place to stay than the two-room apartment with community bathroom they had found. Dismayed at the prospects, Denzel made a promise.

"Just let me make a payday," he said, "and we'll go somewhere else, one way or another."

An Oft-Told Tale

Perhaps it was the fact that one did not easily give up an oil field job. Or maybe it was the friendly people, some of whom they had known in Louisiana, all in the same boat, or that Denzel fit right into his new job with abilities that were needed here where oil activity was perking up fast for the war effort. Probably it was all of these factors plus this remarkable young woman's mode of finding hope and happiness nearly anywhere she was, but by the end of the month, they had decided not to go anywhere right then. By the next Christmas, they were firmly settled in to rear three children and both finish out their days in Crane.

That old story is oft repeated in oil field towns, and Crane is filled with folks who stayed into retirement in the place where they were figuratively dragged. Or merchants and the like who came because they were needed by those the oil had drawn. Some of their children are still here, and that includes the black folks.

Folks like Bill Hollins, who came because an old acquaintance telephoned him in Sulphur Springs. Leon Neeley asked whether Bill had a wife yet. The answer was no. Leon's next admonition, I think most would agree, was a wise one.

"Well, get one and come on out," he said. "I have a good job for you."[14] That was the beginning of a family of fine citizens, as Bill and his wife then reared three children and lived out the rest of their days here. And Jack Lane, whose story is told later in this work: when he found himself stranded in Crane, he took a job and sent for his wife, Sammi Belle, and they reared a large family of good citizens.

According to undocumented lore, the first group of blacks, with a mule team, was brought by Vernon Stell, a Crane automobile dealer. The team and drivers were needed for "mudding" in the oil field.

As the black gold passing through the community poured out a wealth of taxes even at the lowest rates, this soon became a wealthy little town with few wealthy people. Swimming pools, community halls, and parks were all free to residents and their out-of-town guests. A super-large (for the size enrollment), state-of-the-art brick high school building constructed in the forties was featured in a national magazine. The courthouse and most other buildings were well constructed of rock and mortar.

Still, this was a southern community with implicit southern mores, and blacks were seldom if ever employed in the oil fields, so in the beginning it was a white society taking root on a big, flat white rock. But soon there were the more menial jobs allowed to people of color.

Builders needed laborers who worked for much less than the skilled oil field men, and of course the homes of some of those white folks needed housekeepers/housecleaners/babysitters.

Not many places eastward were booming. Small wonder that the black population were relatively satisfied and determined not to rock any boats in those days. Like the Anglos, they were glad to have a job—any job—and most jobs here were preferable to what they, too, had left eastward.

Since I was born three years after this town and arrived here some quarter century later, for input on what it was like before we came I rely on folks mostly in my own generation—or not far behind—who had grown up and attended school here. Their memories and insights after the fact are marvelously sensitive and perceptive.

There was more volunteer input from and about whites than blacks, and white kids of that time have themselves been astonished to realize how we were. One would have to be a septuagenarian or older and of southern upbringing to know that a stone wall is no more—and maybe less—than a river, a railroad track, or even a certain road that served the same purpose throughout the South and Southwest.

Indeed, a friend recently told me of a black section that had been just beyond the pale of one Texas town, and then when the town grew out and around that section, the area was still clearly defined by only four streets. No whites lived inside, and no blacks lived outside that square, though it was surrounded by other, newer neighborhoods.

This puts one in mind of a good mime, who can make an audience see an invisible wall through which no one can pass. Still very real, psychologically.

My childhood was two or three generations removed from the Civil War. I'm not proud of it but must tell that my mother once boasted that her grandmother as a young girl had owned ten slaves.

"Imagine," Mother would say, citing this as a mark of wealth and pride, "ten of her own!"

Maybe because slaves lived away from the owners' houses, we can infer that when they were freed, it seemed natural to some that they kept—and were kept—to their own neighborhoods. That, then, became a ready-made scenario for hatred and denigration by some and separation by all. I cannot explain how or why it carried to my generation; I only know that it did, and so does nearly everyone else my age.

In my own childhood home and in the homes of my friends and extended family, I heard no harsh or mean talk about the *colored* people, but no matter how much I loved a couple of black women who worked for us, they still had to come in at our back door. I guess we were taught by example, or if we questioned, were told only, "Well, that's the way it is."

Crane memories—from childhood and then teenage years—vary according to many things, but the most noticeable factor is where the white young people lived. Most of them were not drivers, were not allowed to cross the highway even on their bicycles, and so spent these years in school and church and their neighborhoods, in a day of no computers and few telephones, when kids went outside to find or make their own entertainment.

Three Communities and a Hub

Strange as it may seem, in a town of under five thousand, to think of three minitowns, this seems the best way to understand our populace and their perspectives. The community was—and is—centered in a big plus sign formed by the crossing of Highways 385 and 329. The northwest quadrant holds the football and baseball fields, community hall, parks, swimming pools, black community, and as of the Park Addition—location of small but nice and well-built FHA-insured homes. And as that addition was built, so was Colored Town, as it was called, in the farthest northwest corner. Today's city maps name part of that area the Hollins Addition.

In the east sections were mostly supply businesses, such as trucking companies, lumber yards, and equipment yards. In the southwest quadrant were all three white schools, teacher housing, the courthouse, and City Hall, beside the water tower. Residences were scattered about all these areas, some even on the highways alongside or above businesses.

Then to understand the multitude of concepts voiced by residents of those days, we must remember that the black community had since the late forties been in the *far northwest corner* of that northwest quadrant, and the largest concentration of white/Anglo residents was in the *far southeast*, just beyond the city limits.

East of Highway 385 and nearly a mile south of Crane's city limits sign was the Gulf Oil Camp, almost a town unto itself but incorporated into Crane circa 1950. The Gulf neighborhood contained—besides family residences and bunkhouses for single/transient employees—a recreation hall, park complete with baseball field and tennis courts, grocery store, and offices, in the manner of most sizeable oil company camps of the time.

After oil companies began liquidating their camps as such, this area went into the city limits as the Mountain View Addition, with many of the same families staying put but now owning their own homes.

As the crow flies, Gulf Camp cum Mountain View Addition is as far removed from the northwest corner as possible to still be in the same town.

Small wonder that the camp kids knew little or nothing of the black community, also largely self-contained. And what white youngsters did know of racial dividers let them assume everyone wanted it that way—the way it had always been.

So three people groups to understand would be the town people, the camp people, and the black people, with distinctively different memories coming from the children of each group. Some folks who came here as young adults are quoted too, but time's a-passing, and many of those are physically gone, some having left us since I started this work.

This seems like another good place to remind readers that this is an admittedly subjective work. Relatively little documentation is supplied in chapters such as this. Any conclusions are my own, unless they are in direct quotations and properly attributed/referenced. This may be called *pre*primary research—live research, never to appear in historical or sociological writings unless by someone down the road who comes to the Crane Oral History Archives to find these quotes to read or to listen to. Then they may call it *primary* research.

Town Kids

Johnny Ward, class of '66, learned about that far corner of town from playmates soon after his family moved to Crane from Graham, Texas. He told of it in an e-mail:

> We lived [in the northwest part of town]. Our neighbors were Junior Guinn and Chris Jones, who lived across the street, and a block down were Kenneth Harris and Leroy Seabourn. Since none of us were old enough to drive, bicycles were our mode of transportation.
>
> During our first week while new friends were showing me around, we came upon the Wall and the Bethune School. I asked about both of them and was told that was the "Colored School" and colored part of town. Well, I started down to the school, going past the wall. The other kids stopped and hollered that I couldn't go in there. Since I had played baseball with the Colored kids in Graham both in their neighborhood and mine, I still didn't think anything about going there. That day I met the Walker boys, the Morris boys, Billy Van and his older Jones cousins, plus a little shy black kid named Tommy Jones. Nobody threatened me or offered to

harm me (except my Mother later when she found out), and I was told to come back any time.

After about three months in Crane, we moved next door to [Paul and Marge. Patterson] on Vivian [in the new Park Addition], and lived there until I left Crane. Several times I was invited to play basketball with the black kids at Bethune, and I did so at every opportunity.

Later I worked at the ice house for Max and Bernice and then for Vance Martin after he bought the business. I made several deliveries to the café/tavern called the Dew-Drop Inn, inside the Wall. Most of the black people I saw in there either I knew or they knew of me. I never ever felt out of place or that I shouldn't be there, because the people treated me as well as did any of the white people I knew.

[Now back at Graham, Johnny recently wrote a familiar perspective of his generation.]

"Now to end this I will say that one of the Colored kids that I played Little League baseball with here in Graham when I was eight years old (I am now 64) is still my best friend today. When I tell him about Crane, he always says, 'Crane must have been a helluva place to have left such an impression on you.' Folks, Crane was a Helluva place, as he puts it, and still is."[15]

Yes. And one "helluva" thing is how many residents of those days vary in their memories and understanding of segregation, but nearly all, black and white, say they are glad of their upbringing.

Little League was a preintegration arena for children's natural inclination to accept one another as people, with common age and interests, not common skin color, being factors of friendship.

Who wants a wall on a playground?

A number of former Crane students recalled the fun of playing Little League ball with the children from the black neighborhood. Several told proudly of their fathers' work with the teams.

Judy Glover Googins is a remarkable Crane graduate from the sixties who put herself through medical school after she became a single mother. Her story can acquaint readers with her parents who, like others black and white but more courageous than some, set the stage for race relations the way they ought to be.

She remembers her father's Little League teams. In her blog, "Songs in the Night," she said she had a completely unprejudiced home atmosphere:

> My "new father," Harry Harmon, married my mom [Shirley], when I was four years old and gave us a new name. With his name we also inherited his reputation. I am thankful to say it was a good one, but even more importantly, Dad, along with other coaches, helped to change the attitude in a community by standing up for the rights of Afro-American and Hispanic people who lived there.
>
> I was not aware of his rare influence until a few years ago when Mom told me about how he had been among the Little League coaches who insisted that every child who wanted to play on a team should be allowed to do so, regardless of race. Then only a few days ago I learned how their courage helped to change an entire generation of Crane children. We moved to Crane in 1959 when Dad accepted a job with Texaco. I was getting ready to start first grade and had a new baby sister who occupied a lot of my mom's time. Dad had fixed up an old bike for me, and I was free to roam within limits. Having come from an isolated Pegasus Gas Camp where there was next to nothing to do, I was delighted to explore the modern, two-story public library, swimming pools with swimming and diving lessons offered at no cost, and free summer recreation programs for kids—all free of charge to residents and even their guests from other towns.

Dad was excited about the Little League and Pony League games and Golden Glove boxing as well as the Crane High School football, baseball, and basketball teams. He was quite the sports fan. As a family we joined the First Baptist Church where my young parents, at only twenty-five and twenty-six years of age, became actively involved in teaching the youth. Mom also became a working member of the Women's Missionary Union, participating in mission efforts both at home and abroad. She was well aware that mission fields exist in our own back yards. Before long Dad was coaching Little League or Pony League teams and helping with Golden Gloves, and Mom was having the young people over for cocoa and her homemade giant sugar cookies. The swimming pools were located at our city park, the summer recreation programs were held at the exhibition hall nearby, and the baseball games were at the fields just north of that. We lived up the road on Elizabeth Street, and I was allowed to walk from our house on hot summer afternoons to the swimming pools and the park, where there were other activities. We often had picnics near croquet courts also free to the public. Behind those croquet courts, baseball fields, and city park was a long stone and mortar wall, which I always assumed was just the boundary line of the park. Beyond that was the section of town where most of the "colored folks" (as we called them then) lived. The black boys would walk across from their neighborhood to participate in Little League games. We were often in that part of town for the baseball games or because some of the poor folks lived there, as Mom and Dad were frequently helping a family in need, black or white, who were down on their luck. I noticed that there was another school

(Bethune) and even another swimming pool in that part of town. It seemed odd, but it was understood that those were the places where the coloreds went to school and swam. However, there were no separate [Little League] ball fields to keep the races apart. Once Dad started coaching Little League, he was eager to have all kinds of kids playing on his teams. He himself had grown up poor, the youngest of nine children reared by a widowed mother, and he was not a practitioner of racial or social prejudice. Even though schools were not yet integrated in Crane, Dad chose interracial teams. Dad's team performed well, and a few of his players became some of Crane's best athletes. Other coaches also led the way with integrated teams.

When I tagged along with Dad to practices and games, I got to know the guys on his teams. They probably don't remember me, but I admired them and ran after their foul balls when they knocked them out of the park. Some of those balls even rolled over by "the Wall."

[During games Judy and other children could retrieve and take balls to the concession stand for free snow cones.]

It's funny how the kids on the teams didn't seem to have any problem getting along with each other. Racial blending of Little League teams helped smooth the path for integration in Crane public schools [and elsewhere], and I am proud of my dad for being a catalyst of this change.

That stone wall behind the ball fields, I discovered recently, was not a boundary for the park but a reminder of the hard-held beliefs of some of the town leaders that the blacks should be kept in their place and separate from the white folks and their children.

> I had never been aware that the wall was intended [for segregation]. It certainly didn't serve that purpose for my dad's team members, the Little League baseball teams, or for us as a family. By the time we were in high school, I think that most of my generation were oblivious to the wall's purported meaning—but perhaps I speak only for the white kids. Nevertheless, it never entered into our conversations, and both Afro-American and Hispanic kids became my friends.

Concurrence with Judy's views and interpretations appeared in an e-mail from Randy Robbins, who had been on her dad's Little League team, and whose own dad also coached these integrated teams.

> After living in the world away from Crane, I soon realized that men like Vance's dad [Cecil Gibson], my dad [Jeff Robbins, for whom Crane's Little league Park is named], and Harry Harmon were ahead of their time in trying to change attitudes. Such fathers and coaches contributed to my generation's hatred of injustice and an enduring belief in the value of character over any physical identifying characteristic.

Young people of those days express memories from many perspectives, but all have a tone of wonder as they look back and reassess the times.

Eddy Dean Smith—now Dr. Eddy Smith—lived in northwest Crane, by his father's bar near the black community. His random memories include one of the few stories of racial cruelty I have heard, though we can infer from some things *not* said that there were more.

"My father, J. L. Smith, used to sell beer to African Americans from the back door of our bar. I remember hearing my father tell the story [from before my memory] of an African American being beaten in our parking lot one night. I have no idea why it happened."

Bobby Tillman, class of 1969, had an eye-opener when he got to high school.

> I remember the wall, or at least something there that separated the "colored" section of town from the rest. But that was one part of town I never went into—that is, until I joined the Crane Industrial Arts Club.
>
> [Sponsor] Mr. Bill Mayes had us help the Lion's Club sell mops and brooms. "Oh, my goodness, we had to go into Colored Town!" I went with Mr. Chrane (high school math teacher and member of Lions Club), however, who had been there many times before, and I was actually surprised. Don't know why, but I was. The folks knew him. They were nice to him and to me.
>
> I remember school integration, just as I started high school. Going into high school was in itself a big step. Now, added to that was the fear of being around those "other folks."
>
> Once again, how mistaken I was! Billy Van Jones, Tommy Jones, Thomas Morris, and on and on—how could we have not known about all these folks? They were wonderful friends. If people of all the races were as fine as those of the black community in Crane, the world would be a much better place.

How could he have not known? My guess is that it was a nominal conforming to the established mores by Bobby's parents and my generation, beginning to see the light but not self-assured enough to do much about it. Because I knew Bobby's parents, both teachers, I feel—though I do not know—there would have been no prejudicial talk in that home. Then with integration they became, like most teachers I know, implementers of what they had always privately known was right.

Linda Chrane Chamales, class of 1963, said her dad, Doug Chrane, was one who always did what he could, and she wrote recently about that.

> I guess my dad's attitude and that of so many of our teachers and mentors in Crane had a big impact on all of our beliefs as we grew up. Daddy was also responsible for bringing or arranging for someone else to bring Billy Van Jones and his grandmother to the church with us for many years. Until a couple of years ago, I never knew the wall existed; my parents never mentioned it.
>
> Daddy was a fan of Duffy Neal. He thought Duffy could fix anything that had to do with cars, and they spent many hours talking about and working on the restoration of Dad's old green 1950 Ford.[16]

Dyantha Green was one of the white town kids whose dad "was as likely to drink beer at the Dew-Drop Inn as at the Driller's Club or the Airport Drive-in," she said. She told of their family's coming to Crane just after the oil boom began, in 1937, willing to "make do" with makeshift living conditions during their first decade here.

> My dad came, not to work in the oil fields, but to work building houses, the first one being one for us to live in. One of those tin shanties on McElroy Street was ours at first. There were whites as well as blacks without sewage or water. My dad hauled water as did many, in the '30s, and when we did get indoor plumbing we had a cesspool, but we had a neighbor who had an outhouse into the early '40s.
>
> My dad helped put up the rock wall at the cemetery, and he built the first bank building in 1948. He may have helped build that wall on Gloria Street too. But for whatever reason the wall was built, my parents were never prejudiced, and neither are their children.
>
> I don't think I ever thought about the fact that the blacks couldn't go to school with us, just knew that they didn't. I still wonder whether students attending Bethune School had any less opportunity

for, or quality of, education than the students at other Crane schools.

Camp Kids

Families in oil camps lacked one problem of others in this new town: housing difficulty. Some, like the Weisers, didn't get into the camp at first and rented or bought houses, often "make-do" living places. But when their names came up for a camp house, they knew they were set. The company provided utilities and kept the houses in repair, painting them regularly.

There were some twenty-five-plus oil company camps throughout the county[17]—all within the Crane school district—but the Gulf camp almost adjacent to town was the largest, a distinctive part of the community and yet with a camaraderie and citizenship of its own.

And oil camp families had perhaps as much kinship with folks in other camps as with those in town, especially "oil field children"— as they were called, almost derogatorily, in some contexts.[18] The children seemed all like siblings or cousins. Many had known one another in other oil industry locations, and there was a relationship reminiscent of army camps, with company bosses having the better houses and their families having slightly higher social status, but that was not a thing that disrupted the family atmosphere of the whole camp—of camps in West Texas, in the world, anywhere oil field workmen brought their families with them.

Never having lived in an oil camp—or even, while growing up, knowing anything about them—I learned of them from literally hundreds of now grown-up camp kids. And after years of this input, I am still waiting for the first negative comment about an oil camp childhood.

Some of these "kids" in Crane have expressed dismay to find out what they hadn't known then about segregation and the wall, but nearly always that is qualified by not blaming anyone and by an open mind and heart when they found out.

Norma Horne Kachelmyer, class of 1956, and her family, including three sisters, lived in the Gulf Camp. She said that as a child she never saw the wall or that northwest corner of town. She wrote an e-mail recently from Romania, where she and her husband are missionaries.

> I never personally met a black person until my college years when I worked at the Corner Drug during summers. There was an elderly black janitor working there named Bruster Nix. He was a very nice man and we became friends. One day I gave him a milkshake (my gift) and was shocked when he sat down in the phone booth to eat it. That was my first encounter with segregation "rules."
>
> I had never wondered about the separation of races. It was just the way things were, and it never occurred to me that they might even want to go to school with us.

Hardly any black people worked in the oil field, according to memories e-mailed by Jim Agnew, class of 1963.

> I think two [black] men drove a vacuum truck. The only association we had with the black people growing up was in summer baseball and going to the Dew-Drop Inn. They did not have the best housing by any means, but I believe they were happy. We all got along as far as I know back in those days.
>
> I guess I thought at that time that blacks did not want to integrate any more than whites did.
>
> I hope I am not too wrong in my remembrance of this, but during the days of LBJ and integration, some Midland people with a black integration organization drove two busloads of blacks to Crane and parked in front of the white swimming pools. Their purpose

was to upset the way that Crane people were living with each other. The Crane blacks met the buses and would not let the Midlanders get off.

Don Womack, class of '56, wrote that he doesn't recall a thing about the wall, but a related memory is clear. He told how he had admired high school principal C. A. Carroll for his handling the situation when a Mexican family arrived in town, with the first Hispanic children to be in high school.

> Mr. Carroll came on the intercom and announced the impending arrival of the Pena family. I don't remember all his words, but classmates I have talked with remember the same thing: Mr. Carroll said, "Some of the children will be your classmates, and you will behave and treat this family with respect." And we did. We were good kids and probably didn't need Mr. Carroll to remind us, but he did, and I am sure Mr. Brady Nix [superintendent] said, "Amen, C.A." What a town and what a school.

Don and many of his old friends often exchange tales of camp life on *Purple and Gold Nuggets*, a Crane e-mail news line chaired by Fredda Bishop Arney. It's easy to see the great memories they have of camp life.

A sweet informal essay by Karen Howell Keith hangs on the wall of a West Texas café.[19] It expresses the family feel of oil camps, even for children who moved frequently with the same company.

She wrote that the camp kid had a special world.

> A world that was a haven, a sanctuary, a retreat. No matter if it was in Monahans [Texas] or Algeria, a Camp Kid could always find a home, food, love. Just because her family worked for the mutual company.

Just because she was a Camp Kid ... and we were family.

The camp kid understood moving was a way of life. It didn't matter where you went. You had instant friends to make sure the first day in the new school wasn't so scary. Someone would show you everything. Classrooms, cafeterias, even bathrooms, just in case. Someone would greet you to make sure you got on the right bus going home, 'cause sometimes it could be a 20-mile walk.

Town or oil camp, school, church, playtime—all made memories mostly pleasant in this place and school too small for social divisions but just right for individual attention in nearly all ways. Most felt part of one big family—the white kids, that is.

Things were similar but different for the black kids. They too seem to have felt secure and protected within their community. For various reasons—newspaper coverage of white school activity, names of people for whom their parents worked, contact with all-white city and county officials, and the like—the black children were a little more aware of the white kids than vice versa.

A sidebar here: At a recent funeral in Wink, Texas, my husband served as pallbearer with a black man who had graduated—from the black school, of course—about the same time as Charles graduated from Wink High. He later told me he was amazed and sorrowful to hear that this black man knew about Charles's football and other accomplishments and to realize how little Charles had known or cared about those kids in that "other" school.

Road from Odessa to Crane, 1941 (Photo by Mary Ruth Weiser)

Southbound side of road from Odessa to Crane [northbound lanes across median to left], 2012

LEFT: Taken in Gulf Camp: view south c. February, 1942; ABOVE, view east from park on 21st Street c. summer 1942 (Photos by Mary Ruth Weiser)

13 Karen Howard Keith, "Camp Kid," unpublished essay written for her parents, 2000.
14 Sue Neeley Christon, *My Times*, unpublished manuscript, March 2013.
15 Johnny Ward, "The Crane Wall," in *Come All You Cranes, Do You Recall ...*, ed. by Sue Hudson Marines (Omaha, Nebraska: self-published), 202–203.
16 Linda Chrane Chamales, "The Crane Wall," in *Come All you Cranes, Do You Recall ...*, ed. by Susie Hudson Marines (Omaha: self-published, 2011), 203.
17 Ken Daniel, ed. *Crane County Oilfield Camps, 1926–65* (San Angelo, Texas: self-published, 2014), 2.
18 Estha Briscoe Stowe, *Oil Field Child, Number Seven in the Chisholm Trail Series* (Fort Worth: Texas Christian University, 1989), 2.
19 Karen Howard Keith, "Camp Kid," unpublished essay.

READER'S NOTES

Train a child in the way he should go: and when he is old, he will not depart from it.
—Proverbs 22:6 KJV

Children, obey your parents in all things: for this is well pleasing unto the Lord.
—Colossians 3:20 KJV

Honour thy father and thy mother: that thy days may be long upon the land which the Lord thy God giveth thee.
—Exodus 20:12 KJV

The way things are is the way things are.
—Chipmunk "chorus" in the movie *Babe*[20]

Chapter 3

THE WAYS WE WERE— BLACK KIDS AND THE HUB

LIKE CAMP KIDS, YOUNGSTERS IN THE Bethune community felt safe, protected, and loved. Each group was in his little "village," though the analogy isn't a complete one: both groups were taught traditional courtesy and a general deference to adults, but the Bethune kids generally had parents who trained them in a different kind of deference for anyone white, anywhere.

These parents too had come west for better opportunities than what they had left. And with immense faith and optimism, they prepared their children for the better day they knew would come.

Far Northwest

Estiene Bishop knew about better opportunities. She said she and some of her family had moved here in 1938, and she told how it happened.

> My cousin Tootsie, he wrote my mother a letter and told her that if she came here, she could get a job working for twenty-five cents an hour. My brothers, Louie Jones and Otto Jones, and my stepfather could get a job working at the dairy. I didn't know it then, but I know it now—that dairy was right across the street from where I live right now.
>
> When I came to Crane, there were three other black families here. One of them was Tommy and Reba Vaughn. Then one was my uncle George, my cousin Tootsie (Walter Gerald—you all know him and his wife). Two of our charter members, Bill and Viola Hollins, had come December 26, 1937.
>
> Those people are gone now; I'm the only one here to tell this story, and I want it to go down in history. I want all of you here, from Crane, born in Crane, raised in Crane, to know the facts about Crane black history. And as the Lord would have it, right behind me is where Mount Zion was organized—through First Baptist Church. They had a Sunday school building over there on McElroy, and they let us use it so Reverend Hollins could have church. And that's where we organized.
>
> There was one Spanish family, and they lived on the ranch. There was no Spanish people whatever in the town, and not too many white people. There was nothing but pasture here where we live now. No houses—just pasture all around, everywhere. I grew up with Crane.[21]

Black children by law had to be educated, and Crane officials at first transported them to a neighboring town, former student Herman Vaughn said.

But when the black population grew, Crane ISD gave them first-class facilities too—better than those even for white children in many towns eastward. Brick buildings were soon built for the Mary McLeod Bethune School—a smaller building than other schools, as the black student population was smaller than the white.

Here by Accident

The need for work brought Jack Lane to West Texas, but actually the town and the job snagged him as he came through from Tahoka, where "the people were really nice but there just wasn't enough work year-round." He was headed for McCamey where, an old friend had written, a job was available. Leaving his wife and two children in Tahoka until he could check on it, he took the bus for McCamey. Many stops along the way made for slow travel. The last stop before McCamey was Crane. It was late afternoon, and he was very hungry, so he got off the bus to find something to eat.

He spied a Chili Parlor nearby, but since he couldn't enter the front made a half-block run around to the back. He found friendly people and was eagerly devouring a great bowl of chili when through the front at the window he saw his bus pulling out.

"I didn't know what I would do next," he said, "but Sheriff Jack Young was in the front and must have guessed my situation."

Young came back, asked some details, and then sent Lane to Vernon Stell's garage. This was 1944, wartime, and cars were scarce for Stell's Ford dealership to market, so he had added a garage as well as a clay-grinding shop to produce mud for the oil field.

After a short conversation—maybe a little work—Stell offered Jack a job, and not just for that day. Jack called the friend in McCamey.

"Then I worked there twenty-one years," he said, "before I put in my own garage."[22]

So Jack and Sammi Belle Lane and their fourteen children became good citizens of Crane instead of McCamey.

Maybe we should thank that runaway bus.

The Move across Town

At first the Lane family lived in a tent where most of the other blacks had settled. They were squatters of a sort, with no ownership of land, no utilities or other basics. Jack remembers exactly where his tent was: in deluxe irony, it was on the southeast corner of the block where the Faith in Christ Church, pastored by Jack and Sammi's son Ellis, is located today.

Though no one can be very specific, when the area was being prepared for the Park Addition project, several who had been here in the forties spoke of seeing some houses being jacked up and literally moved across town to the northwest corner.

It is not hearsay but a certifiable fact that with the move many blacks gained ownership of land and their own homes, with electricity, sewage, and running water. That's when the infamous wall came into the picture.

Bissinger had said that nobody outside the fence much cared what went on behind it.[23] Well, that was all right with the folks behind it. According to those grown-up children today, they did not need or want much outside help, thank you very much. This corner of town, like an oil camp, was virtually self-sufficient: here life for old and young centered around the school and church, the swimming pool and the basketball court. Adults had the Dew-Drop for dining out or for fellowship over a drink. Some left the area for their work or to go visiting *out of town*, and young people finishing school mostly left Crane for better opportunities of all kinds. But families seem to have found early security in this home base.

Memories of those preintegration days in the northwest corner vary, but the input I received was mostly positive, from a minister's early observation of a pleasant place to grown-up children's memories of caring teachers and supportive parents. Only a few blacks spoke of the wrong kind of leniency by some teachers and discrimination of the darker kind, but even those expressed appreciation, at this twenty-first-century part of their lives, for the village that really did raise the child.

Training Up a Child "by Hand"

At the dedication of the Bethune School marker, Brother H. A. Bowens had spoken of his pleasure at coming to this "nice little town" and noted the firm discipline of children, even in church. Such a good thing, he said, for the children's future.

In nearly every interview, discipline for a good reason showed up as a recurring theme of family life in northwest Crane.

Cookie Lane said all children were expected to be involved in whatever was going on in the community.

"Our teachers went to church, so they knew if we went. We had to be in Sunday school, we had to be in church, all of that—you didn't rate high at school if you didn't do these things."

And not rating high meant facing retribution. Most parents set an example, but also, like Pip in Dickens's *Great Expectations,* children were raised "by hand"—applied to the seat of the pants. Most information on these tactics came from the Lane siblings, but others bore it out.

When I noticed the ease with which most of the black students came into CHS respectfully and courteously, I formed a question that I eventually started asking: how did parents like the Hollinses, Joneses, and Neals—to name just a few—bring their children up to be deferential and almost servile to whites as expected in a segregated society, and then, when we integrated, still handle themselves with courtesy, grace, and dignity? These wise and farsighted parents—what was their secret?

What I learned defied all currently accepted theories about child rearing, child abuse, and the like. It was a kind of tough love—very tough. Clarity and consistency of attitudes and actions by the parents made for a childhood that turned out adults who love and appreciate their parents. Of course there are many things even my best black friends may never tell me, but there is no mistaking how these children of the fifties and sixties feel about their upbringing. They consistently express appreciation of their parents, they take care of aging and ill parents, and they even joke about their rearing: "I told Mom I should have turned her in for child abuse."

"We knew exactly what we could and couldn't do and exactly what the retribution would be if we crossed the line." Thus I was told many times.

My friend Margaret, now of Amherst, Massachusetts, but once—for two years in childhood—a citizen of Crane, was almost aghast when she and I chatted with Cookie on the subject.

Cookie's answer about how their parents prepared them for getting along nearly anywhere was quick:

"Mama's ironing cord," she said, and vowed the predictable punishment came for everything from not doing their school work to not behaving on the school playground, and even not doing their best on the basketball court.

With an expression flashing from smiles to frowns, Cookie told of rule enforcement at school.

> Miss Neblett, our first principal, was very, very strict. We had a set of swings on the playground. Now the boys could pump, but the girls wore dresses, so they weren't allowed to stand in the swings and pump. But on a weekend when she was gone, we got in those swings with our dresses on, and we, oh, just pumped away. But she had a spy out. Come Monday morning, that person gave Miss Neblett the name of every girl that pumped in those swings, and we got a whipping. For pumping—now that's true. And if you got a whipping at school, when you got home—that was double trouble.

Close tabs were kept on all processes at school. There was no such thing as not getting a teacher's note home to parents. Parents and the teachers worked together.

"You don't give a note when you get home, the parents know it immediately," Cookie said. "I thought they had spies themselves—how did Mother know that I got a note today to bring home and I didn't bring it? I didn't see the teacher come home with me. But she knew it, and if you didn't—you paid the price."

A universally enforced rule in the Bethune community was "no-pass, no-play." Cookie smiled at the thought that such a furor was made in CHS and elsewhere in Texas when the University Interscholastic League instituted that policy in the eighties, and told of Bethune's policy.

> Mr. Hall was the coach, and he didn't care how good you were. If you didn't pass, you didn't get to play, and all we really had was basketball. So you hustled to get your grades. We always had that at Bethune. If we didn't pass our grades, we didn't play ball—and that was all we had to play.
>
> Whenever it was time for us to go to a tournament or something, Professor Hall would go from house to house making sure everybody was in bed by nine o'clock as he had ordered, and the parents agreed with whatever he said.
>
> But those were glorious days to me.

I heard such comments often in telling of those days, not only by Cookie. Undoubtedly one reason for this perspective is a saying Cookie told of among black people: "We're going to whip you now so that you won't be pistol-whipped later."

She remembered a time when her mother was going to punish her and some of her siblings a little differently.

> Instead of whipping us because we didn't do our homework, she wasn't going to let us girls go to a tournament. We got the word back to Mr. Hall, and, well, he went to our house and consulted with Mother and got her to agree to let us go to play because they really needed us. (Sometimes there were four or five Lanes on the team, and if we left, they might as well forfeit the game.) So he got her to let us go, but then when we got home that night—well, punishment had not gone away.

Cookie's brother Ellis Lane replied to the same question: how did your parents bring you up to know enough not to get in trouble, in or out of the community? He grinned a little as he answered.

> Child abuse. They beat the hell out of you. No, "Go to your room." Yeah, boy, I tell you that is not playing, you know. Adults demanded respect. Children didn't enter a room or other space where grown folks were there talking, unless they were called. And, boy, if you crossed that line—they tell you in a minute, boy, you don't have—you don't have rights. You got to do what you're told.

Both Lane parents seem to have set examples—practiced what they preached, consistently—but Jack has confessed that he had left the discipline up to Sammi. That appears to have been the case in other families: the fathers worked long and hard to make the living, and the mothers were the disciplinarians, though most of them also worked for pay, mostly at housekeeping.

Obedience Morphs into Honor

"But you still grew up loving them," I said, and Ellis grinned again.

"Yeah, oh yes, I'm telling you the more they made you respect them, the more you loved them. Like right now, my sisters Johnnie and Cookie live at home with my mom, and they're taking care of her like she was a baby. She does nothing, you know, just thinks it done, and it's done—and the same with our daddy."

So as children they had to obey but grew up to honor willingly the people who had brought them through this sociological tough time with the toughest love.

They heard stories of their parents' tougher, earlier times, like this one from Terry Neal.

> My dad never rocked the boat, and he always told me, "Don't rock the boat." Later on in life, I asked my mother, "Why is Daddy so afraid of white people?" Mother said that in Gilmer, Texas, a white lady was raped. They found a black man in the vicinity, and they put it on him and hung him. They cut his testicles and penis off, and they stuck 'em in his mouth. They drug him behind a Model T with a chain around his neck as an example for all the black people to know not to mess with white women. It was terrible. I'd hate to see anybody go through what some of those people had to go through.

Not only their parents but all adults in the community felt obligated to correct behavior of the young.

"If I did something wrong at a friend's house," Ellis said, "those parents got me right then and there and then called my home. I got it again when I got home." Seemingly the whole community wanted all children to have built-in protection of good behavior for inside and outside that wall, Ellis and Terry and others said. So parenting was universal.

But community nurturing also included the gentle, caring side.

"Then if you were at somebody else's house at lunchtime, you went in there and you ate just like at home," Ellis told. "It was just

THE WALL THAT FAILED

a community of people that respected each other. I know it was because of the hardship they shared."

Discipline occasionally required the cooperation of people outside the community.

Obviously thinking they had outgrown some of those rules and accountability, three or four boys robbed the Dew-Drop Inn, taking a few steaks and some beer "to have a great party," according to Jimmy Finley.

Identification and apprehension came sooner than expected, though, and then three of them were in county jail. Soon one mother came to visit them, carrying a large purse.

"I should have known Mama had something in that bag," Jimmy Finley told when a group discussed it at a recent reunion. She did, and the sheriff was quick to comply with her request.

"Just give me a few minutes with them."

He let her into the cell with the boys. There she pulled out that something, her ironing cord, and proceeded to whip each boy soundly. A Crane Northwest problem, solved in the Crane Northwest way, seems to have worked.

> "Being in jail was bad enough, but then getting that whipping was not manly," Jimmy said in a recent interview. He assured me the lesson worked, and he never stole again. Like others who grew up in the Bethune community, he said that discipline was pretty severe but never arbitrary.
>
> "We knew exactly what we could do and what we couldn't do," he said, "and exactly what the consequences were if we stepped out of line. Of course that did not keep us from getting out of line, and we sometimes took that chance, but if any adult caught us, we were not surprised at the result."[24]

Also like many others, Jimmy said he had "a wonderful childhood in Crane."

At age four he had decided to follow his siblings and friends when school started that September, and at first his parents would have detained him. But the teachers said, "Let him try it." He tried it, he learned, and later graduated a year or two ahead of others the same age.

A graduate of the Bethune School before integration, Finley then graduated with a math degree from Prairie View A&M, taught school for a time and "did not like it," then returned to school to become a registered nurse. That was his favorite career, he said. Recently retired from a truck-driving job with a local oil company, he has kept up his nursing certification and said that's what he would do if he decided to go back to work.

Yes, the hardship made the bond throughout every home and other entities, not the least of which was the school.

Teachers were regarded with respect and love. Brother Bowens had spoken of Professor Hall, also basketball coach, who "put something in those boys."

Billy Joe Neal, his wife, Inola Hollins Neal, her brother Don Hollins, and I discussed those days and the teachers who made students feel they could do anything. Bill said he was reluctant to integrate.

> I didn't really want to go [to the integrated school]. I enjoyed Bethune because the people encouraged you to—I guess you say reach for the stars. They told us you can do anything you want to do. They—we all—knew our parents were just right down the street, so when they told us something, they meant it. But they actually cared.
>
> For a time we had two grades in a room, because there were not that many students. It was a relaxed atmosphere. There was no pressure, no agenda by anybody. So I really felt I learned a lot. Because of the way they made me feel at an early age, I thought I wanted to be a doctor, but all that changed about 1966.

He too saw basketball as a unifying factor and knew the tough but loving supervision helped make them seem safe and secure. He recalled going on a bus to Big Spring for a Bethune game.

"They could put nearly the whole community on buses and take us to games," he said.

"Certain places the bus was not allowed to stop for us to eat. I was a small child, but I paid attention to things like that, and they knew whether places would accept us or would reject us."

So the adults were careful where they went, and the children had their memories of carefree times. All their procedures were strict but predictable and consistent as the discipline.

Though she attended there only through the third grade, Inola too said she loved Bethune and did not want to integrate. She told of her first exciting day and other enjoyment.

> My father, Bill Hollins, was a janitor at Bethune, and he walked me to my first class in the first grade.
>
> There were four children in my class. I don't know—we were just in our little world. Like Don and Bill said, the teachers just made you feel you could be anything you wanted to be.
>
> I was the only girl, and I was an A student. I was just happy. It was fun and carefree. I liked the teachers. I was in the Coronation of Favorites, and I sang a lot during those three years, and I just liked it.
>
> When we had to integrate, I was devastated, and that is the truth. I feel we should have had counseling, because I was actually traumatized. My first few years—I guess from fourth grade, I probably say, through sixth grade, seventh grade, I don't know—it just took a lot of adjusting.

Inola's brother Don, a few years older, also told of great preintegration days at Bethune.

> Classes were small, so we got the needed attention. A lot of our elementary teachers been teaching twenty-five, thirty, thirty-five years, so we learned a lot about life from them, and they had been in the system long enough to know how to teach.
>
> School was preparing me for life, and at different points later it all came back. I realized what they were doing. It was a grand experience.
>
> Oftentimes I wonder what I could have become. That change of schools is not the only reason. Other issues changed my life, but at Bethune they gave us a sense of pride, and at that time it was kind of unheard of, but we felt that we could be anything we wanted to be. You know, within our world that's what we were taught. You got to believe in yourself, and the whole community pitched in and helped you. It's unlike any other thing that I can explain.

Don reflected that classes with two grades in each made for mutual help. He told how it worked.

> My class was one of the larger ones—eight students, and we kind of pulled together and helped each other, you know. If there was a problem in math, that one just didn't quite get, we would all help, and before the day was over, everyone knew how to do that problem.
>
> Our teacher had fifth and sixth grade, so while he was teaching the other grade, ours would get a little group and show each other how we did it and help them figure out their own ways. Everybody had to get over the hump or learn it before we could go on.

As he told this, I was thinking that is how group work should operate, and how much teacher monitoring it had taken in some of my classes of all-white students to see that group work didn't involve just copying from the "egghead." Case in point for smaller classes everywhere.

So in the northwest corner, children heeded parental warnings not to venture alone from that community and its school and church, and when they did go out with their parents, they minded about which water fountains to use, where to sit at ball games and theaters, and other such rules that seemed to them to be "just the way things were."

Adults sometimes went to town, with or without their children, to shop or to use the washaterias, and they modeled how to "keep their places."

Blacks could go to the movie too, but sit in the balcony. That must have been just another familiar degradation to the older blacks, but to the kids, it was fun to be with their own school friends—and even brought envy from some whites. One former student told me that the blacks always had an advantage in the pickle fights, and one had asked her parents, "Why do the black kids get to sit up there?" Louie responded to that with a smirk.

"We liked it," he said, "'cause we could throw things down on you."

Two milk carton tops could get one into a Saturday matinee at the Crane Theater, state of the art in 1950s. White ushers, mostly teenagers, of course had their hands full, but they seemed to enjoy it too. I guess I get a little wistful, myself, remembering how we who lived too far away for children to walk never hesitated to leave children for a movie and come back for them when it was over. The ushers and popcorn boys would look after children waiting for their parents after the matinee.

That was just the way things were. Young people, black and white, dealt with what was, and many say they thought that was the way everyone wanted it. They didn't know why and didn't seem to care.

Dorothy Abron Brown, who attended Bethune through the eighth grade, recalled school days in the black community. She made me smile as she told about winter mornings, about community discipline, and days that were fun even as the students accepted disadvantages.

> I remember those many days of walking to school. Mother always cleaned us up and we put Vaseline on our legs to moisten our dry skin because black people's skin gets a little ashy. And walking to school when the wind was up, we were full of sand by the time we'd get to school, so we'd have to clean the sand off before we'd go into class. But those were fun days.
>
> We'd always wear dresses, but we'd have on long coats, and we'd kind of squat as we walked to cover our legs, and a lot of times the wind would just blow right through you. But those were great times to me.

The whole community reared the children, and all adults corrected all children's behavior even while caring for other needs, Dorothy continued.

> I believe we need that now, but nowadays you can't say anything to anybody's child for fear of the parent or even the child. But then everybody guided the children, and we were good people. I really wish that we could have those days back.
>
> We never were limited on the amount of literature that we received, but we always got the used books, after they were finished or got new books at the white schools. We'd always see different names and see who'd had the books before.
>
> One thing that I regret, though, is not getting a lot of black history because books from the white schools were limited on that. Our instructors gave us a bit of our black history but not a lot. We didn't

know about some great black people that did great things, like the Buffalo Soldiers.

But we had excellent teachers, and they worked with you until the light came on. They worked with you, and you did things repetitiously, and everybody learned. This no-kid-left-behind policy, to me it's not good, to push kids along. Bethune teachers worked with the students, and they were not left behind. It's a matter of taking that time, taking that little extra time for the students to understand what's going on. We had that.

At the Hub

Meanwhile, remembering the way it was takes Sue Christon to a whole different world from most of her peers, white or black. She started her life virtually at the hub of Crane, the center of the plus sign, the crossing of the two highways. She spent her first twelve years in the Neeley Hotel, on the northwest corner of the highway intersection, owned and operated by her parents—mostly by her mother, as her father's time was devoted to building in, and promoting of, Crane.

Sue's associates were folks who stayed in the hotel—some transient and some semipermanent—and children who lived in small rentals near the hotel. Occasionally she had a chance to play with ranchers like the Barnsley children, when they came with their mother to spend a few days in town.

But the hotel was not a place where many children were allowed to play or visit. Sue never noticed or thought about their absence until years afterward, when she realized the hub of business and transients and speculators probably was not deemed a proper place for most children.

But life was too busy and full to think of that. She had pastimes and playmates.

From the time she was little more than a toddler, in after-school hours and all through the long summer days, she tried to take every step her daddy took, unless she was following in the footsteps of her beloved Mable [Williams, later Taylor]. She played in and around construction sites, making cement bricks, even painting—whatever Leon would let her do. When he was out of town or otherwise busy elsewhere, she was under the watchful care of her mother and especially Mable. She loves to recount those days, how Mable was her caring friend, how Sue's mother also looked out for Mable, and what a fascinating time it was for a little girl.

> I was a very loved and protected child of the forties and fifties, in a world of her own.
>
> Part of this protection, from how things really were and how people really felt and what was really going on, came from a lovely colored lady who worked in our hotel. Mable was mine.
>
> Mable was from the old way. As whites would say, she knew her place. For example, she would eat with me, but she would not sit to eat with Mother and Daddy even though she was asked many times.
>
> Mother looked after Mable's interest, and that too seemed natural. Once she sent a guest packing after he had made lewd advances to Mable, and another time she made some drunken young men clean up their own "puke" before Mable would clean their rooms and bathroom.
>
> When Mable came down that day and told how some soldiers' rooms looked upstairs, my ears perked up, and I trudged up just behind the women to watch the fireworks.
>
> That was something to see. Those poor guys would clean a while and puke a while, but Mother was standing over them to see it done right.[25]

Mable was not to be abused in that hotel.

Several black friends have acknowledged similar relationships, before and through the transitional days of integration, wherein a white, usually an older adult, would communicate without words to a black that his communication with, and help of, that black would extend only so far as not to arouse ire of more prejudiced whites, ire that might prevent more help.

Mores and standards were made for whites' convenience. Though it was not okay for a black woman to sit down at the table with whites, that same woman caring for a child could sit down at the table with that child, or take the child with her to a black neighborhood on a semiofficial errand, or go with the child into another white area for similar reasons.

Sue spent long hours with Mable, she said.

> I spent a lot of time following Mable around while she was working at the hotel. We talked—I can't tell you what about—more with feelings than words. I was influenced by her more than by any of the whites around me, even my parents. Part of this love came in the form of discipline, as she treated me like her own, I thought. I now know my life was not the real life around me. There were two worlds, mine and Mable's. I loved to go to Mable's house and to the Dew-Drop Inn, where I loved the feelings I sensed and the laughter I heard. I always wanted to stay all night at her house, but she wouldn't let me. I was not a part of her world and never would be.
>
> Children are not born with prejudice. They are taught this from parents or others, and life all around them. Mable was not the only colored person who kept my world from the truth about themselves and the whites.
>
> Like Bill Hollins—(hold on, here it comes) "N--- Bill," we called him—I don't know how to make

> people understand the feeling behind those words of endearment as they were spoken then, and understand this love. I guess if my daddy had a brother, it was Bill. But Daddy is gone, and so is Bill, so maybe we will never know the whole truth about that relationship.[26]

But Sue had a seat in that little world where two men could be true friends, work together as equals while both knew they were not equals outside that door. Where each could/would keep his proper place in the view of other whites and blacks.

> I do know Daddy respected Bill as a man, not just as a colored man. Bill and Viola lived behind the hotel. Viola was a beautiful woman. James was my age, and he had a little sister—Inola—we liked to tease. Mother cried for two days when they lost their twin babies.
>
> I now know that for generations back, the blacks were beaten down, taught to know their *place*. Mandy recently said she would have liked to ask a white man, "Where is my place?" But she didn't.
>
> I too would want to ask a question of my black friends at that time: how many whites knew how you really felt and what you really thought? You never let us into your world. I think this is even true today. Does this come from generations of fear and hate?

Undoubtedly so. But how will we ever know?

From my background, growing up in Corpus Christi, I recall that people of Mexican descent, though they attended school with us and worked with us, were almost as discriminated against as blacks. My parents dearly loved a Mexican man named Joe, who worked in Daddy's store. They took a special interest in Joe and his family and even helped with the education of his children—but still, a younger, less experienced white man was promoted over Joe to assistant manager, and that man later told me Daddy had admonished him to correct Joe more often. I tell this with shame but with admiration for Joe, who maintained his dignity, his grace under pressure, to the eventual betterment of himself and his family.

In several years of extensive visits with relatives and close friends in Mississippi, I saw similar relationships. All these put me in mind of an oft-repeated saying, especially during integration struggles: "Northerners love blacks as a race but hate them as individuals, while southerners hate them as a race but love them as individuals."

So it was in my home. We kids loved our babysitter Annie Mae, a large black woman of *Gone with the Wind* style; we would snuggle in her arms as easily as anyone's and would have gotten in trouble for talking back to her as to any adult. But she had to come in through the back door.

That's just the way it was.

Sue reflected on generational perspectives.

> Some of my generation and older in recent years have talked about how their children could not understand how this could have happened. How they could let it happen. I guess, though, the human spirit is a very frightening thing, fragile thing. No one could understand how the Germans could have done [or allowed what was done] to the Jews or why, but it did happen, and the world went on. This was the way it was for me in the forties and fifties.

But some things would change overnight. Sue told of James Hollins, a playmate and fellow worker, as she helped her daddy in those days.

> James and I were close. We played when we were little 'cause they lived behind our hotel, and there was a week's difference in our age. Then when Daddy was building our new house, in '48, when James and

I were growing up but technically too young to be driving, we were anyway. Daddy had us cleaning the bricks from a building somewhere in town. That means getting the concrete, the mortar, off them so they're bricks again. We spent all summer cleaning those bricks and putting them in Daddy's old pickup and driving back and forth from town to the new house and unloading them. That was the last time James and I were really together.

It isn't hard to picture Bill Hollins and Leon Neeley, looking at those two budding adolescents as they drove back and forth in the truck, laughing and having natural fun. The two fathers could see what comments might come from blacks and whites in the community and—perhaps without words—agreed it was time to stop this innocent childhood relationship before those children were irreparably hurt by that world beyond theirs. Sue said she just didn't see James again.

I just didn't ever see him again, and after I got older and got into some of this [history] stuff, I realized Daddy and Bill had decided we were too old to be seen together, you know. I imagine it had caused stirs already. Mother and Daddy never said anything to me about it, and I guess Bill never said anything to James, but that was the end of it. We had been like brother and sister. But now it was, it was just over with.

With the move to Second Street, into that brand-new house it had taken Daddy two years and three army barracks to build, my life changed. I was no longer a downtown kid who lived and played in the hotel and in the caliche holes Daddy dug for sewer lines and building foundations. I had new playmates— children who hadn't been allowed to come to where I lived to play with me before. The black people around before, I now saw only occasionally, when I needed something at the hotel or was with Daddy working. So I still tried to spend a lot of time with him just to see my old playmates/friends.

Soon the Neeley girl and her school friends were of the driving generation and better able to stay in after-hours touch with others in the rest of Crane town and the Gulf and other oil company camps.

These places and friends did not include the Bethune neighborhood or its inhabitants.

Most of the front yard of the Neeley home—which has been through several owners since those days—is still paved with bricks Sue and James hauled in the old pickup from the torn-down buildings. It undoubtedly was a showplace in the north part of town, adjacent to the equally new but smaller houses in the Park Addition. They of course were built of new lumber according to FHA specifications, whereas the Neeley home, like many other buildings in towns like Crane, were constructed from barracks available at army and air force bases being dismantled now that the war was over.

Sue Neeley and Tommy Christon were married in the spacious living room of the new home, with the reception catered by the Dew-Drop Inn. She begged Mable to sit as an honored guest on the front row, but that best friend chose to watch the ceremony from a doorway.

"We had a corsage for her and everything," Sue said, "but she just stood and watched."

So there the town was. Most adults were apparently happy to be better off than they might be or had been elsewhere, children blissfully unaware of what might have been or should have been. For all they knew, it suited everyone that those black people lived over there, we lived here, for whatever reason people lived where they did. Not a matter to be contemplated.

When my husband and I moved to Crane in the fall of 1955, a year after the Supreme Court ruled against it in the famous *Brown* case in

Topeka, segregation was still the norm and ostensibly peaceable—in the town of just under four thousand.

Everything was boomtown luxurious, supposedly according to population, under the old "separate-but-equal" code, with all public facilities county-maintained and free of charge. There were four well-built school buildings: Crane Elementary, Crane Junior High School (later Middle School), Crane High School, and the twelve-grade Bethune School for blacks.

Teachers in all schools were on the same pay scale, based on certification and experience, roughly 30 percent higher than in the South Texas schools where we had taught before. Each school had its own library and librarian, cafeteria, gym, and playground.

When I remember Crane in the fifties, it is through a series of vignettes:

- Friendly people everywhere, glad to see the new teachers.
- Children playing on all the playgrounds after school and on weekends.
- Courteous black people coming in the back door of small cafés, or stepping to one side for me at the post office or drugstore counter.
- Smiling black children watching ball games.
- Two big, husky black teenage boys ambling down the dusty side of the asphalt-topped road from their neighborhood toward town, in the middle of a summer day. All the white boys I knew of that age were working—college students in the oil field, high school boys in the grocery stores and similar businesses. These fellows probably would like to have had a job, too, I thought at the time. Of course they would, I would learn some forty years later.
- Separate seating at athletic events for blacks, for baseball just below second base and for football at one end of each side. Blacks living only in one section of town did not seem so out of the ordinary to me, as every Texas town I had known anything about had such a separation.

THE WALL THAT FAILED

Yes, segregation was alive and well—more "well" for blacks than in many other Texas places, I'd wager.

In an area north of Fourth Street were several blocks of small, new five-room houses—the only part of town that might appear to have zoning, the Park Addition of FHA-insured homes. Actual zoning was probably never considered in this mushrooming town that had begun as a tent-and-shack camp, but a zoning of sorts was required for these new houses to have government-approved loans.

In childhood, I had experienced very little contact with colored people. We didn't go to school with them, didn't live near any of them. I recall a couple of delivery boys who worked in my dad's store, just boys, only a little older than I. My mother worked in the store, too, and my brothers and I had several different black babysitters, and, for a time, a sweet young black woman named Mosie came to help Mother with the ironing.

I was vaguely uncomfortable with their having to come into our house through the back door. And when I rode a city bus, I was uncomfortable that adult women were standing up at the back of the bus while I, a child, was sitting down near the front.

I now believe that discomfort was common in my generation, no matter what we were taught and how we were required to behave. And I'm sure that latent unrest/guilt had fermented within and made us ready for integration after others had done the risky work for us. People like Martin Luther King and Rosa Parks and the myriad white supporters of integrated education. We didn't have their courage, but we quietly admired it even as we expressed doubts about whether that were "the way to go about it." We shed tears when Emett Till paid the ultimate price in Mississippi, not for being a feisty kid but for being a feisty *black* kid. We were saddened by the assassination of Medgar Evers, whose motto was "Violence is not the way."

Our fair and practical side knew this situation needed to change, not only in the name of humanity but also in the name of patriotism and common sense. Call it an enlightened selfishness: how can any nation be at its best while putting down and virtually out of commission the talents of such a large part of the population? How could we be so long seeing and acting on that?

But we were.

Change in the Sixties

I wish I could say that, when the first desegregation ruling came down, Crane America stepped right up and obeyed the law. Not so. As a community—or as the school board represented us—we weren't exactly dragged kicking and screaming into doing the right thing, but we did quietly dig in our heels until the irresistible force came.

Perhaps that position of resistance came from the independence brought by our community wealth: Crane schools had never accepted federal funds and so had escaped many federal regulations. Children whose families could show need received free lunches from the district. Gym clothes were free to all students; athletic teams were furnished full uniforms, including appropriate shoes for each sport. Adequate and updated science apparatus, playground fittings, library books, virtually everything we needed—or any staff member *thought* we needed—was supplied from local funds.

It was the same, at least to outward appearance—for the black school. By grace of the oil companies, local homeowners' taxes and even utilities were low, low, salaries were high, high, teacher pay was tops in the state, and school buildings state of the art. Not one dollar of federal funds needed.

Small wonder we virtually declared our autonomy and distance from federal strings, at least by default. For a violation of law to be corrected, someone must bring suit, and who would upset this bird nest on the ground? Not I, I'm afraid, though like most teachers—I now believe—I knew that segregation was wrong, that "separate *but equal*" had never been more than a half truth. Not the black teachers, though they surely knew that it would be best for their students. But privately, they probably knew also that few if any of them would be hired in the integrated schools. And they were right.

THE WALL THAT FAILED

In the fifties, it seemed Crane whites took pride in their arrangements with blacks. And blacks at least gave the face of being satisfied with their lot—after all, it was much better than most had come from and could have easily been made worse by a "bad attitude" on their part. That initial twenty-five cents per hour for household labor increased a little with the boom. Not many towns were booming during the Depression years, and not many places burgeoned so as war became American reality. There was little or no joblessness in Crane.

So when federal integration orders came, no black person was dissatisfied enough with the status quo to risk losing even what they had by rocking the boat. And no white person feeling guilty or courageous enough to risk censure from fellows.

In the early sixties, all Texas knew integration was here. The subject was in headlines throughout the state. In Crane, there was much talk at the school board, in school, downtown, and in homes, but it is difficult to find a printed word for documentation of the subject. It seemed that everyone was waiting to see what "they"—whoever that was—would do about it.

No one set up any protest for or against the law, no one tried to show reasons we did or didn't need to integrate, and no one said anything *officially* at all. That worked for a while. This was, after all, small potatoes compared with metropolitan areas such as Dallas/Fort Worth—and even smaller cities such as our neighbors Midland/Odessa—where furors raged over redistricting, bussing, and the like. The powers that were, in Crane, resisted integration in all the default ways. We just lay low and waited as if to see whether the matter would go away.

Finally, over a decade after the Supreme Court ordered that all schools carry out the intent of the Topeka ruling "with all deliberate speed," the tide reached us: we had to make a plan "or else."

On September 16, 1965, the following paragraph was contained in the middle of the school board minutes, as printed in the local weekly newspaper.

Superintendent W.A. Miller told the board that the school's plan of integration had been amended and was now acceptable ... A letter to parents next year will contain the following statement: Anyone not registering a choice by Aug. 3 must file a choice-of-school form ... If the form is not received, the student will be assigned to a school ... without regard to race, color, or national origin.

Jim Bortzfield recently gave a student's-eye view of events.

"In the spring of 1965, we students were sent home with a sheet of paper asking which school each student wanted to attend as a part of desegregation as ordered by the government.

"Of course, all the black kids picked the 'big' school. That was our first year with them," Jim said.

Not quite all of them. Bethune would remain in operation for the school year of 1965/66, and students had the option of attending either place. When choices were all in, this had the effect of closing the secondary part of Bethune. Only grades one through six remained in operation there. For one year.

Six of the younger black children stayed at Bethune that year. Maybe that was because some parents desired to give them time to get ready, or to keep them close for another year, but underlying the decision was a humanity that Bucilla Abron Bowens told me of years later, while we were waiting for her husband, H. A. Bowens, to begin the marker dedication program in August 2005.

"Brother Bowens had asked if we would let [my daughter] Joyce and some of that group stay here," she said, "so that Professor Jones would have some students."

Thus these parents gave a beloved teacher a job for another year. There would be no place for Professor Jones in the reorganized and newly integrated school.

"All the older ones went to Crane High School," Bucilla said, "but not all the younger ones, but one year later all of them went down there. Yeah, I've seen a lot."

The beaming and tolerant and upbeat smile with which she told this is a known characteristic of hers. It's a smile that has always reflected hardship but understanding and eternal faith that the Lord will provide. And when we can, we must do our part by following His commands about patience and kindness.

The following year, there was no Bethune School, only the Bethune Annex, which has been used since as a locale for our cosmetology department, auto mechanics, and sometimes, kindergarten classes.

Delights—and Heartbreaks—Ahead

From my perspective, integration began in the fall of 1965, when some twenty-two black students enrolled in Crane High School. There was no fanfare, no confrontation, no outward dismay, and no visible tension except from a straining on nearly everyone's part to make this work. We were to have some of the successes we hoped for, as well as some of the disappointments we feared.

I believe that most educators were more than ready to make integration work. It is to our credit and our shame that often we know what is right to do but can't quite do it until someone with more courage forges out, gets called a radical, and maybe is personally maligned for taking a stand. Then our aching consciences have us ready and eager to do the right thing.

Yes, we were more ready than most of our powers that be knew, but it was a readiness within a cacophony of fears and hopes, apprehensions and expectancy, not unlike that of a play cast on opening night. We were poised and ready to get this show on the road. We would have several days or weeks or months of opening-day jitters.

ABOVE: View west on Sixth Street (Highway 329) from Gaston (Highway 385): Neeley Hotel on right, City Hall/Water Department on left, with Courthouse beyond. (BELOW): View toward crossroads from front of City Hall on Sixth Street. (Both photos by Mary Ruth Weiser, c. 1942)

---

20 Chipmunk "Chorus," *Babe*. Produced by George Miller, directed by Chris Noonan (1995, Universal Studios).
21 Bishop.
22 Jack Lane.
23 Bissinger, *Friday Night Lights*, 59.
24 Jimmy Finley, conversation.
25 Sue Neeley Christon, *My Times*. Stanton Texas: unpublished document, 2012
26 Sue Neeley Christon, "Colored People," unpublished essay, Stanton, Texas, January 2008.

READER'S NOTES

III

THE PLOT

What a delight it has been to follow their story and to have lived so much of it with them. Like some of the students I interviewed, I found the folks of Bethune to be wonderful friends, and so they are still.

Jesus loves the little children,
All the children of the world.
Red, brown, yellow, black and white,
They are precious in His sight.
Jesus loves the little children of the world.

—Classic children's hymn

Chapter 4

OPENING-DAY JITTERS

"R<small>ED *AND* YELLOW, BLACK AND WHITE</small>, they are precious in His sight," my generation of children sang in Sunday school. The *brown* was added in my children's generation, for "Red, *brown*, yellow, black, and white," with the same rhythm. But if I loved Jesus and those black folks loved Jesus, why did our color difference override other courtesies I had been taught, like giving my seat to an older person? I had sometimes wondered—but silently.

So I grew up in the guilty-but-hesitant generation.

And when the integration orders reached us with a legal nudge, most Crane educators—like most decent people across the South—acted on what they already knew was right.

We had felt the vague uneasiness of knowing that "equal" part of the old ruling wasn't quite so. Relieved to be part of righting a wrong we'd never quite had the courage to oppose before, we welcomed the chance to change.

Well, most of us. A few—particularly some administrators—said, "Those kids don't want to come over here until they have to." Wishful thinking, perhaps, to delay dealing with the situation, or maybe those guys just didn't have teachers' hearts or didn't know what they didn't know.

Picking up Their Options

Charles Stroder was the assistant principal and director of student activities in Crane High School when integration started, and he told of some educators' views.

> It was believed by some that the kids were not coming, as they had an option that first year, but I privately disagreed. And sure enough, to some folks' surprise, that first day or two of registration, they trickled in. One came bringing his records, and then two, and finally the rest flooded in.
>
> I knew some black and white kids already knew one another, had played Little League ball together, and I had associated with some of them that way, so I didn't anticipate any problems. Still there was tenseness because nearly everyone was trying to do the right thing—teachers, students, administrators, custodians, black kids, and white kids—but we needed to be sure what the right thing *was*.

Early Middle School Days

Nearly everyone here remembers the first days of integration. Bethune student Louie Jones and Crane Middle School student Annette Lopez Lane, who became acquainted in middle school at that time and were in my high school journalism classes later, were explicit in their recollections some forty years after the fact. We have all been good friends ever since their high school days, so when I took on the segregation/integration in our museum's Oral History Project, these two seemed naturals for my first interviews, as we'd had similar conversations before, just hadn't recorded them. This conversation later became a program for the Permian Historical Association and an article in the PHS Annual. The thought of changing schools was at first "scary" for Louie, he said.

> It was exciting too to approach something different, wondering how things were going to be, and wondering if they were going to be better. Knowing my classmates were going with me gave me a good feeling.
>
> That first year, you know, we had an option—stay [at Bethune] or go—but from the beginning it was understood that Billy Van, my cousin who lived with us, and I were going. My mother and grandmother never considered anything else. We were going to Crane High and Crane Middle School, and that was that.

Annette said she was just excited.

> I thought it was about time. I was born a flower child, always the peace-loving person. My father worked with Pink Hollins, and my father always complained that they couldn't go into restaurants the normal way, because Pink had to go in the back. So my dad

would go in the back of the restaurants with him. Coming from a Hispanic family—my birth father was Caucasian, so I was half-white and half-Hispanic—I embraced the chance of letting another culture into my life. I really did, and wound up marrying a black man, A.J. Lane—Louie's uncle.

I was very happy about integration and made friends right away. I remember standing outside that first day at junior high when the bus drove up. Mrs. Gothard, our physical education teacher, helped us organize a little welcoming committee, to cheer the new arrivals, to let everybody know we were not opposed in any way.

Some experiences were on the humorous side. Annette recalled being lab partner in home economics with Etta Morris.

"We laughed and cut up and made mistakes together and laughed some more," she said. "But I think I made a D minus in that class."

One "goof" still brings a smile to Louie's face.

I am not sure whether it was the first day, but we were all standing on the [northeast corner] of the middle school building. No one told us we had to go over there, but that seemed a safe haven for us. Most of the white kids were by the front door, at the other end of the block, or in back of the school. But we congregated in that area by the steps. For some reason, there was not a bell—or we couldn't hear it—over there.

And after lunch we had been there—oh, I guess ten or fifteen minutes after the bell when some teacher heard us outside her classroom and came and told us lunch time was over, and it was time to get back to classes. We thought that was funny. We were going to play all afternoon, I guess. We continued to go there every day after lunch, because most ate in the cafeteria together. But we listened more carefully for the bell.

We changed finally and joined the other kids. I guess we just needed to be together for the first two or three weeks, to adjust, and to get into the flow.

I cannot remember an incident when kids were mean. Maybe I haven't thought about it, or—I can't remember any harshness. I'm sure there probably was, because it was as new to the white kids as it was to us. I remember telling them that I couldn't get everyone's name straight, because—well, coming from a little community—[Annette interrupted here, "We all looked alike!"—and Louie grinned.]

Uh-huh. It was a kind of a reverse thing. Some were blue-eyed and blonde, and some were brunette, and still I couldn't tell them apart. That is so often said about my race, you all look alike, but truly, to me they did. I'd call one another's name. But we finally got to the point where we could have easy conversation.

"I think there was a kind of shyness," Annette said, "with meeting new people. I don't think there was any animosity." Louie agreed.

Right, no animosity but a new, strange feeling. But by end of the year—or before—I felt very much a part of the middle school. I accepted it as mine. In my mind, everything was okay. We all got through it, and I have lifelong friends that I met then.

A little white boy, Mike McKay, and I were inseparable. And a Hispanic, Jessie Esquivel—Mike, Louie, and Jessie—we were great friends, on into high school, and even after graduation we'd meet and visit in someone's town.

We are friends to this day, and it all began at Crane Middle School.

A Negative Remembered

Not all first-day memories are pleasant. Billy Joe Neal's was the nightmare some had feared.

> Mother pulled up to the front on the east side of the building. Those old cars then had the real big, long doors, and I set my supply box down to close the door. She had told us all, "No matter what they say, you just keep walking, but now if they put their hands on you, you can defend yourself. But words—you just keep going." I said, "Yes, ma'am," and that's the way it was going to be.
>
> But after I shut the car door and turned around, I got hit in the nose by a boy who said, "You're not welcome here." Well, I was in a fight, and Mama wasn't even around the corner yet. I had been there ten minutes and was in the principal's office for fighting. Some kids around said I started the fight. So the office people called my mother. We both got licks for that. It made just a lot of tension on my part. Later [during the day] a release came with physical education class and sports. There at least I could get rid of some of the stress, but I couldn't wait to get back home.

And Another, Later That Year

Philosophies and politics were many and varied in those days, and in spite of good intentions could not be kept out of the school. It's a

THE WALL THAT FAILED

wonder yet—and, I believe, a tribute to certain people—that we got past what could be considered the worst controversy that first year.

Years later, Louie Jones told it best. Though he had no memory of students or adults who were mean to him, he well remembered the higher-up decision causing pain to many.

> My cousin Billy Van had gone eleven years to Bethune, and his last year was the year they integrated. Billy Van had always been very smart, and had made As all the way through school. I can remember just one time at Bethune he got a B, in choir, and he was so terribly, terribly upset.
>
> I was glad to get a B in anything. I even felt blessed to get a C. But I had a good singing voice, and singing was kinda second nature to me. Billy couldn't carry a tune in a bucket—really—and he knows he can't. He was Church of Christ, and he did not sing to instrumental music in praise services. That's a part of their belief. But that B hurt.
>
> When we integrated, people had heard about him, that he was an A student. And they said, "We'll see whether he can hang with the white kids." Again, he just blasted them away and was still an A student. In fact, by the end of the year, he still had the highest grade point average in his class.
>
> But when it came time to name the valedictorian, he was looked over.

The time he referred to is well remembered by many educators of the time. I never knew—or cared to know—whose decision it was that Billy Van did not qualify for the valedictory spot, what kind of distorted rationalization was used, but it could not have happened without the consent of the seven-member school board. Yes, the handbook said the valedictorian had to have gone to CHS for four years. Why hadn't he done that? Because he was not allowed to. So did "separate but equal" not mean "equivalent"? The predictability of that decision still hurts and must have taken a big measure of grace for the people affected to handle. I daresay the ones who made/approved the decision are not proud of it today.

"Everybody in our community was terribly, terribly upset," Louie said. "That is the most prejudiced activity that stands out in my mind. It made a real division between whites and blacks." He said his grandmother went to the school to talk with the superintendent.

She had raised Billy Van from a little boy, Louie said, and when Louie's father died, the grandmother and Billy Van moved in with Louie and his mother. They were all close.

"What upset them upset me," Louie said.

"I don't remember how it all turned out, but I know that he did not receive those honors. Oh, I think he prayed. He was on the stage at graduation, and he was allowed to pray."

Allowed to pray. He did so graciously. What class he and his family showed that night.

Decades later, when I was doing that first paper for the Mosaic of Texas Cultures, I called Dr. Billy Van Jones, professor at Abilene Christian University. After I asked about his final average, he said he didn't remember. I inferred that he didn't care to remember, that his mind and life were focused on more important things now.

Help from a True Educator

Billy Joe did tell of a bright spot a few days into the transitional year. It had to do with a special kind of teacher—a real pro, I like to say—who found ways to help him.

> I had a terrible speech impediment, and when we had to read aloud, the white kids they thought that I couldn't read, but then my reading teacher, Mrs. [Amanda "Mimi"] Wilkinson, noticed something. We would take spelling tests, and I aced those, but when time

came to read aloud, I couldn't. She started watching me and figured it out. She called me aside one day and said, "You have a speech impediment, don't you?"

She then had ways to deal with that by adjusting my oral reading requirements. Another teacher might not have picked up on that.

Other teachers told of some early insights. One math teacher found business as usual: teaching is teaching and kids are kids, no matter what color.

"I had three of the Bethune kids in the same algebra class, and after a couple of weeks I realized nothing was different. One was very, very intelligent and hardworking (went on to obtain a PhD and teach in college). One was an average, hardworking kid, had to work for his grades, and one just didn't want to work—*didn't* work. Same types as those I'd been teaching for years."

Yes, professional teachers have always known how to tailor teaching applications for individual differences, long before special education, mainstreaming, and the like were in our vocabulary.

Remember the Cranes

Often, as high school goes, so goes the whole school system, especially in small towns with one high school, where children of all ages grow up almost idolizing the older athletes and wearing the mascot emblem and following the teams. A legacy from the Bethune School provided just the talent spice needed for that tendency.

When I saw the movie *Remember the Titans*, based on a true story of a southern high school where coaches and young people and football smoothed many of the integration bumps of a community, I was reminded of our West Texas parallel to this.

We see the Titan effect when we *remember the Cranes* and their remarkable basketball teams.

In both places, it took official action to bring about legal integration, but the true integration happened in the sports arenas. There young people who know about teamwork sense a truth without verbalizing it: no team, like no country, can be at its best without utilizing everyone's talents. And when young people get acquainted on the court or the field, traditional prejudices of an older generation can mostly be sloughed off.

Since this is a true story, let me admit here that I knew or had heard of a few Crane white parents with attitudes similar to some in the movie. They actively and verbally opposed full integration and even instructed some white children not to help the blacks in their efforts. But, unlike the movie, this work will not be specific about those incidents and people involved, just admit that they existed but move on to accentuate the positive.

Certain forces intrinsic in education, as well as in the nature of young people, were catalysts that mixed and bubbled and made us a unified population at CHS. The family name of one catalyst is *sports*, and its first name is *basketball.*

When I replay the memories of Crane in the late fifties and sixties, none is more vivid than that of basketballs bouncing on the outdoor court of the Bethune School yard any time of the day or night we happened to be passing by. They dribbled and shot, dribbled and shot, boys and men of all ages, and often a few girls.

Volunteer fire fighters told of answering a call to that area late on a chilly winter night, and the neighborhood basketball game was in full swing. All generations were there.

The Bethune Leopards had consistently been champions or close contenders in their conference of all-black schools. Many a white community member—including several coaches—had eagerly attended this local phenomenon's games at the Bethune gym and been graciously welcomed. Usually someone found them a seat of special advantage: no segregated seating there.

George Grounds, who had grown up in Crane and then returned as coach/teacher/counselor, remembers that the Leopards' biggest competition was Colorado City, who also won many championships.

Grounds said he can still hear Willie Morris leading the chant, "All we wants is a hundred."

The atmosphere captured by Estes and Grounds was echoed by many in telling of those days when literally the whole community supported, physically and verbally, this only sport the Bethune students had.

Besides Bill Estes and business teacher Bill Teague, both certified basketball officials, many other white citizens of all ages had gone to the little gym to see this marvel—and, I would guess, to wish we had some of these guys on the CHS team.

Yes, the Bethune basketball team had won three state championships and numerous lesser peak games in their conference of all-black schools. They had had no other competitive sport open to them except, in the fifties, Little League baseball. But two or a dozen could play basketball, and the guys of Bethune had lived the sport.

And thanks to some courageous and farsighted coaches and teachers, many of the black and white kids had already experienced the joys of playing ball together, in the Little League and Pony League.

A First for CHS

So the Leopards became Cranes in the fall of 1965, and that winter the Crane Golden Crane basketball team went to the state finals for the first (and still the only) time ever to date, making the state tournament for only the second time in the school's history.

By carloads and busloads, a big part of the Crane population descended on Austin to see Crane down Rockport 67–43 and then lose to Lake Worth 60–42. Freshman Tommy Jones was the only AA player elected unanimously to the state tournament team.

We had some good white ball players, had had them all along, but everyone knew what new blood really took us to the state tournament. We had the Jones boys. Senior Billy Van Jones, junior Eddie Dee Jones, and freshman Tommy Jones were the only black players on the varsity that first year. Greg Jones was white, and his father, B. J. Jones, had a quick answer when friends teasingly asked him which boy was his son.

"The one on the bench," he said with a grin.

Others on the team—and make no mistake, it was a *team*—were Glenn Fletcher, Gary Gaines (later coach of the Permian Panthers made famous in *Friday Night Lights*), Jerry Grinstead, DeWayne Ervin, Hayne Hamilton, Bob McKay (later College All-American Football Team), Lynn Shelton, and Mike Waggoner. Jack Gothard, later Crane ISD superintendent, was their coach.

Oh, and there was another Jones around. Louie Jones was manager.

When I talked several years ago with Billy Van, his main nostalgic regret was that he hadn't had more time with that team, another year after this one in which they really learned to work together.

What fun it was to watch him on the court. Like each of the players, he had his own style. He was not very tall for a basketball player, but those long, deft arms well made up for any lack of height—helped make an advantage of his stature. He would be buried in a little moving huddle around the opposing player who had the ball, and like a lizard tongue after a fly, those long arms flicked out and back, and here Billy Van would come with the ball, which he dribbled back down the court and put high into the air and into the home basket. Sometimes that seemed to happen before the bulk of players had turned around! I believe he actually reached in and under the other players' arms to twist the ball out but never could watch fast enough, and how I have wished for a game film to run in slow motion.

Readers with a passion for education know what team sports success can do to unify a school, minimize personality differences, and even motivate students to keep their grades up, to *learn*. That's what basketball did for CHS in the winter of '66. It improved dispositions, added fun to the season, and fostered a color-blind camaraderie.

Truly athletics, like music, is its own universal language, and no one speaks it more fluently and fluidly than young people. They relish its coordination, its grace, its rhythm, the occasional cacophony, and frequent crescendo. So do their mentors, teachers who care about the whole person they are trying to develop educationally.

Texas teachers, especially in West Texas, have long known how to use the interest (overemphasis, maybe, but whatever) in sports to educational advantage. "If you can't lick 'em, join 'em" works pretty well. With administrative support and coach-teacher cooperation, many a borderline student has found it within his ability, and advisable, to bring his grades over that borderline to stay eligible for sports.

Off to Austin Again

We have continued to have good basketball teams but have been to the state tournament only once since then, in 1969, when Arlen White was coach and Tommy Jones was a senior. We lost in the semifinals and claimed fourth in state.

Tommy earned his fourth consecutive all-state ranking then and set a state tournament scoring record of ninety-one points in two games. Again, virtually the whole town turned out, making a festive occasion of the trip to Austin. Students attending the game were given excused absences (parental discretion), but this time most teachers had to stay in our classes for most of the day. My husband and I, who had sent our three children on to Austin with friends, listened to the first game on the car radio as we went down, and stopped just before entering the dead area near the hill country to hear the last heartbreaking moments, when the Cranes lost the semifinal game but Tommy received a standing ovation for his record-making final points.

Some of today's young people who didn't know anything about Tommy perk up and take notice when told that, according to a recent issue of *Texas Basketball* magazine, Tommy held the Texas record for single season rebounds from 1968 to 1989, when it was topped by a kid from San Antonio Cole—Shaquille O'Neal.

Tommy's name is found on other state record lists: highest scoring game (twentieth for sixty-five points), third place for highest scoring average (third place for career rebounds, third with 1,677 in 1957–1969), single season scoring (1,425 in 1969), career scoring (2,559 in 1967–1969).

That was while we still had some of the powers from the old Bethune gang, and before—as some town pundits liked to say, only half-jokingly—we corrupted them. Maybe it wasn't a joke, or a regular "corruption." Maybe the myriad of other opportunities newly opened to black students simply diluted their efforts, splintered their concentration. But it became a legendary time, treasured by all who were a part of it, retold (and maybe refurbished) at reunions still.

The '69 team were Ricky Anderegg, Jimmy Burr, Ronnie Gurley, Jackie Jeffery, Tommy Jones, David Morgan, Terry Neal, Billy Owens, Randy Robbins, John Teal, Ronnie Willis, and Benny Wilson. Just being on the traveling team, whether one played or not, was an unmatched treat that was shared with all the junior varsity players. Louie Jones and Tim Atkinson went as managers.

Let this story not give the impression that basketball was the only thing making integration work, nor that all was rosy in this transition.

Other sports helped too. Black players, already good athletes, quickly learned the special moves and nuances of football, and the camaraderie generated in the locker room and practice sessions came out on the fields. The exhilaration felt by black players who had only watched schoolboy football from the "colored" section of the bleachers now seemed to empower them to give the game their all. But now they learned what black professional athletes had faced for years: one could be the hero of the game and still be "just a black guy" off the field. Terry Neal remembers such heartbreak. So the dark must be told with the bright.

After-Game Heartbreak

One Friday night in 1971, the Golden Cranes had a grand victory over their longtime rival McCamey. After the game, fans rushed out on the field, as usual in those days (sadly, that is against UIL rules now) to hug the players, slap their backs, and compliment each on special plays. Terry said he had really felt like a part of something that night, he had arrived as a person, and things were going to be okay. He went home, changed into clean clothes, went up to the homecoming dance—and was refused admission.

The refusal was by a respected citizen. Years later when I recounted this incident to a student who had been a contemporary of Terry's, she gasped, "Who would do that?" Well, we now know that it was done quietly, without fanfare, and cloaked in the most genteel manners by white adults who had been carefully taught about segregation and prejudice all their lives. They hadn't the advantage of being in school and on the baseball fields with other children of all races and finding out that children are children, people are people, whatever color.

There was no girls' basketball at CHS when we first integrated, but the Bethune girls quickly adapted to volleyball, which paralleled the football season. As elsewhere, the usual sports problems were not racial, but the incident Jo Ann Davenport related, of a coach who slapped her—told in the next chapter—might have become an issue in a different time or place.

But it worked for then, or so the principal personnel involved say.

Our retired teachers group—no longer on the front lines but still cheering the troops on—met recently in the old Bethune Building, and Cookie Lane, who had graduated there, took us on a detailed tour of the building as she recounted her own and others' experiences in each room. Lovingly and almost with reverence, I thought.

She brought some memorabilia with her, including brochures from a state-wide celebration in the seventies of black athletic championships. Proudly she told of her part in a great Austin trip.

Like other black history, recognition of black athletes was late in coming—after integration was finally a fact. But it did come, truly better late than never, as most of those players, girls and boys, from the last days of the Bethune School were still alive and able to go to Austin when the University Interscholastic League recognized their accomplishments.

Besides the captioned pictures in the booklet, Cookie showed us glossy team photos from the sixties. Later, when we copied those for our museum archives, I told her we needed IDs—did she have a list? No, but she just sat down and identified from memory every player on some six or seven teams.

Classroom teachers, as well as coaches, have always been pragmatic enough to find their own solutions. The one found by Jo Ann's volleyball coach wasn't tried by anyone else that I know of—I'd say a very good thing—but throughout the regular classrooms, many of us discovered what spice the black students could add, with their upbringing for courtesy, ready sense of humor, and general good nature, and with the acceptance and welcome they felt from most of the white students.

Not all was rosy but perhaps rosier than it might have been had this been a different kind of community. Mostly we all—students and teachers—learned and grew, even suffering through each other's ups and downs, progress and pain.

READER'S NOTES

An old man, going a lone highway,
Came at the evening, cold and gray,
To a chasm, vast and deep and wide,
Through which was flowing a sullen tide.
The old man crossed in the twilight dim—
The sullen stream had no fears for him;
But he turned, when he reached the other side,
And built a bridge to span the tide.

"Old Man," said a fellow pilgrim near,
"You are wasting strength in building here.
Your journey will end with the ending day;
You never again must pass this way.
You have crossed the chasm, deep and wide,
Why build you the bridge at eventide?"

The builder lifted his old gray head.
"Good friend, in the path I have come," he said,
"There followeth after me today
A youth whose feet must pass this way
This chasm that has been naught to me
To that fair-haired youth may a pitfall be.
He, too, must cross in the twilight dim.
Good friend, I am building this bridge for *him*."

—Will Allen Dromgoole, "The Bridge Builder"[27]

Chapter 5

GROWING PAINS AND PLEASURES

S<small>UCCESS OF THE OPENING YEAR OF</small> the new and improved student body of Crane schools was gratifying. Glitches had been fewer than most expected. Still there were heartbreak hurdles ahead as we continued growing. But there were delights ahead too.

Not only teachers/administrators but the total staff—custodians, secretaries, maintenance—all knew it was up to them to set the tones of progress. Well, most did. A few dogs in the manger are found in every mix, and this school was no different. But we did have enough true professionals making on-the-spot decisions to mitigate the effect of the other kind.

And behind all that, we had what can facilitate any educator's effort—parental support. The Bethune community—the village that raised the child—had with their firm but consistent discipline prepared their children for getting along most anywhere.

The Pain-Makers

Not all Crane teachers were secure and professional, and that other kind too made lasting impressions on their students. Billy Joe Neal told of one.

> I remember asking a high school science teacher, "What did George Washington Carver do?" The teacher answered, "Oh, he played with peanuts," and the students laughed, and they went on about their business. Well, I knew right away where I stood.
>
> Also, one teacher would spring tests on us that I knew nothing about. He would ask for homework that somehow I hadn't known about, and I know I couldn't have just missed it. But later I found out that he was one that burnt a cross in our neighborhood along with some students.

Another black student told of a similar teacher who overtly seemed bent on proving him lazy.

I was misunderstanding assignments and making bad grades and asked my biology teacher for any extra help. He said the only time he could give it was at 7:00 a.m. I know he was trying to prove me lazy. But I—with Mother's help—was going to disprove that. She brought me to school every morning *before* 7:00 a.m., and I know I saw a look of surprise when that teacher got there. After only a few days, he said he thought I understood it well enough now.

My grades picked up just enough after that.

I guess so.

The Delight-Makers

Professionals, according to Madeline Hunter, classic education leader, (1) have to make on-the-spot decisions, (2) know things others don't know, and (3) never stop learning. Early days of integration strained our best of all this.

In Crane schools, teachers had long made those on-the-spot decisions ingeniously. Administrators wanting to keep those professional teachers gave them much leeway, or maybe just allowed them take it.

In Crane, America, some folks operated the Crane way to achieve the desired end. While we did see some desired effects as we went, the confirmation had to come from grown-up students years after the fact. Their perspectives as adults who have "been around" and still appreciate their education and their educators—offbeat decisions and all—warms an old teacher's heart. Jo Ann Davenport Littleton told of two of those experiences.

THE WALL THAT FAILED

An Extreme Solution: On-the-Spot Decision

One teacher/coach used what most would definitely be considered far too drastic methods of dealing with interpersonal problems. But that was then and this is now.

This example is best told in Jo Ann's own words.

> The volleyball coach was a hardcore person, and I thought, *Well—her daughter plays volleyball and I know she'll let her daughter get away with murder.* But she slapped her daughter, and then one day she slapped me! I was like—"You can't, you can't hit me like that. I'm gonna tell my mama—white lady, you can't—who do you think you are?"
>
> She said, "Well, you just go tell your mother, but you don't have to. I'm gonna tell her." And she got in her car and went to my house at the same time I did. She said to my mother, "I know Jo Ann can jump higher, and I want Jo Ann to be the best, and she's just half-playing for me, and I won't tolerate it. On my team she'll give 110 percent. I demand the best out of my daughter, and Jo Ann's gonna give me her best."
>
> And my mom said, "Well, I know you wouldn't abuse Jo Ann, and I want what's best for her, so you do whatever." And I was—"Mama, she slapped her daughter more than once!" Mama says, "You know what, it didn't kill that girl." So I was like—"Oh, my gosh."

That solution probably—undoubtedly—wouldn't fly today, but it was a Crane seventies problem, handled in the Crane seventies way. Probably no administrator of that day heard anything about that coach's and parent's on-the-spot decision.

But what did Jo Ann say about it years later?

"I appreciated it. I did."

Tough Love: Knowing What Others Might Not Know

A few years later, Jo Ann found static from another teacher, who countered her "solution" to graduating.

Never known for being quiet and meek, Jo Ann took an aggressive approach when her senior year was imminent. She thought seriously of the one course that had to be passed for graduation, regardless of number of credits—government, taught by only one teacher. She had heard how hard he was, and besides, from dialogue in the halls with him, she was sure he did not like her.

> My junior year, I told my mom, "Get the money together 'cause I'm going to summer school. I am not taking government from Marshall Stovall 'cause he's so tough," and she said, "Well, okay, if that's what you want." And I went to school laughing and said, "Well, Mr. Stovall, you're not going to get me in government class. I already talked to my mama." And he proceeded to call Mom and say, "Jo Ann will not go to summer school; she'll take government because she *can* do the work. She's just lazy, but she can pass if she applies herself."
>
> And I'll never forget coming home that day from volleyball, and Mama said, "Well, you're not going to summer school. You're taking government here your senior year."
>
> "Oh no, Mama, but I'm going to fail and not graduate with my class!" My mama had betrayed me. So I went storming to Mr. Stovall and said, "I don't know why you called my mama. I'm not taking this," and he said, "Yes, or when you go to summer school, it won't be accepted." I was so mad because I had this fear of embarrassment. You know when you say you're from Crane you're somebody, you're apart from everybody else, and very few people

went to Crane Independent School District that didn't graduate. That was a no-no. You graduated, and you went off, and you were somebody. I thought, *I've been elected wittiest for four years, and now the class clown won't graduate.* Oh yeah, I was nervous, nervous.

I said to myself, "I got to sit by the smartest person in the room," and I told Jeb Hughes I had to copy from him. He goes, "Oh, Dugan, you can get it." "No, I can't." And I would be just sitting in class worried about passing, and Jeb said, "Dugan, get your work and quit daydreaming." "No, I'm going to sleep."

"Get your work. You got to apply yourself."

So Jeb was a better friend than Jo Ann knew then. Instead of letting her copy from him or doing homework for her, he pushed her to do what he, like Mr. Stovall, knew she could do. And she did.

Another Crane seventies problem, solved the Crane seventies way.

Again, years down the road, Jo Ann said that experience was good for her, and she credited Mr. Stovall with giving her an interest in politics as an honorable occupation. She has served as a city councilwoman in Odessa and said recently she may even run for mayor.

"I often look back at those days in government class, and I say, 'You know, no cross, no crown,' and that was definitely a cross back then, it was."

Much is said these days in educational circles about dealing with individual differences, and the talk makes me smile. Pros everywhere have always known how to deal with individual differences, and in smaller schools they can.

Mr. Stovall was not going to let Jo Ann slip through the cracks, nor was Jo Ann's mother going to facilitate it. She took Mr. Stovall's word for what he knew about Jo Ann.

EVELYN ROSSLER STRODER

Pro in the Making: Never Stop Learning

It takes a few years' experience for a teacher to become adept, but the caring about what they do—caring enough to keep doing it better—seems to come naturally to many.

Ray Ifera, who had grown up in Odessa, got his first teaching job in Crane in 1968, just after we integrated. He told of beginning in the middle school then.

> I taught Texas history and geography. Crane, like a lot of other West Texas towns, had only about 5 percent black population.
>
> I had two little black girls in one class. We were covering the Civil War and slavery, and at a reference I made to colored people, those girls just bristled at me. I suddenly realized—hey, that's no longer acceptable. So I had to watch myself.
>
> By then we were getting enough news out of the civil rights movements to know that the acceptable term now was *black*. Some were saying *Afro-American*, but black was the favorite term.
>
> Black is beautiful. Be black and be proud. That was beginning to filter into West Texas, and I finally realized that was the way to say it. The term *politically correct* didn't come until 1983. But I understood the concept in the sixties and started teaching myself to use the word *black*.
>
> We didn't have videotapes or the like, and films were ordered from the Region 18 Service Center. But there were old film strips left by the teacher before me, and I got out one on reconstruction and previewed it—showing it on the wall and reading the captions—and was amazed. The Ku Klux Klan was portrayed as the savior of the South, helping restore order in the chaotic period when slavery ended, many

> white people lost the right to vote, and black people suddenly could vote. The social order was totally topsy-turvy until the Klan, according to this film, stepped in.
>
> Really, it reminded me of something I had seen in an old movie produced by B.K. Given around World War I, I believe, called *Birth of a Nation*. It told the story of reconstruction. It looks funny and jerky but was technically the best movie of its time. It was a silent movie, and the captions gave the dialogue, but the message was very clear. The South was in chaos, and the Klan saved the day.

Later Ifera viewed *Of Black America*, a film narrated by Bill Cosby, who was just beginning to be popular, and reports another eye-opener.

> The first part was about how history had been written mainly by white people and history books, especially, before, say, 1950, mentioned black people only in connection with slavery, and without saying anything about their accomplishments. So this story was about how African painters and sculptors in Africa before slavery had created many things copied by other artists like Pablo Picasso and Modigliani. It also told how the first heart surgery was performed by a black man, a black assistant to a doctor, and said black people had been pretty much left out of the history books, or minimized. Then there was talk about the black power movement, of how black children needed to stand up and be proud.
>
> I thought it was a great film, and when I started teaching in high school, I ordered it. But when I showed it, I was amazed at the uproar. I mean it made nearly everybody mad. The black kids became so

angry that they almost walked out of class, and the white kids were angry, also, for the opposite reason. To me it was a good teaching tool, because it got great discussions going. I used it for two or three years, and then I had to stop. People on both sides were complaining.

The principal asked me about it. Videotapes had come out by then, and so I said, "You're welcome to look at it," and so he took the tape. I never got it back. He just was pretty much saying, "Don't use it because it's too controversial."

Ray didn't quit having the discussions and teaching the truth as far as he could see it. This is the position seen often among professionals. Teach with the best materials available unless directly diverted by higher-ups. Then—and Ifera was good at this—still teach the truth you see, any way you can.

West Texas pragmatism.

Word Power

One area of potential misunderstanding and resentment lies in classes where words are our stock-in-trade. My area—specifically language arts and journalism.

Literature has always been a wonderful vehicle, not only for showing life truths but for understanding human nature, beginning with understanding the author's view. ("Pay attention to the words first, whether you agree or not.")

Literature also carries an inherent danger if young people are not guided into seeing what an *author says*, not just what others say *about* his/her *work*.

THE WALL THAT FAILED

Of Denials and Banned Books

Teaching *Huckleberry Finn*, always a challenge, became even more so now. The recurring vendetta against Mark Twain's book—still outlawed in a few schools for its "offensive ethnic language"—seems in the same category with other items in the news that some readers will be too young to remember.

Like when some well-known TV personalities were censured for talking about how whites in slave days "bred" husky black men and women to produce big, strong offspring. That was an indictment of whites, not blacks, but boy did the establishment jump on it as being a racist remark. But I suspect the deep-down reason was that some whites did not want such doings of their forebears acknowledged, and they could hide it behind a self-righteous cloak—just say these guys were insulting blacks.

It's the same shame and denial that made some Crane folks here deny that our Wall between the Races existed. Tear the evidence down, and in a generation or so, folks can believe that it never happened.

Twain, through Huck's eyes, revealed the hypocrisy and posturing of "society" folks, regarding not only race but senseless family feuds and fake dramatic grief. Little wonder some white folks wanted to ban Twain's book. They wanted to break that mirror for what it reflected, without a concern for what was true.

But I tell students we have a little more enlightenment than our ancestors had, partly because of their mistakes, just as our progeny can find enlightenment from our mistakes.

I explain to students about Twain's critics in his own day and how many libraries—like in so-proper Boston—wouldn't even allow the book on their shelves. Some people of the day who "got it" had to accept that some didn't and so be careful with their peers, the same way that whites and blacks who worked together in our days of segregation had to watch their step around the establishment almost everywhere in the United States.

And I used filmstrips by Clifton Fadiman, in which he talks about the N word and Twain's use of it to show Huck's maturing as he learned that Jim was a real human being, not just a piece of property.[28]

Justice Almost Missed

It was in an English class that I had a narrow escape from doing an injustice. We were on a two-day final test schedule with time gaps between the classes, and Don Hollins came in a while before his test was scheduled to ask me whether he might study during that hour and take his test with the next English class. Always a stickler for structure, I didn't ask him why, just said I couldn't do that. He courteously sat down to spend the time left reviewing his notes.

So I have always been thankful that in a few minutes Superintendent C.A. Carroll stopped by the room to ask Don how his father was, and I was shocked to learn that Don had been up all night with his critically ill father. Of course I did an about-face and told him to go study and come back to tomorrow's class for the test.

Many years later, I asked Don about that incident, mainly to apologize for the injustice I had nearly done—or had done, in not asking questions. His answer:

"Well, I really never had a problem, just thought you were doing your job. But when you learned the circumstances and changed, it just endeared you to me for the rest of your life that you let me do that. You became special that day to me, very special."

What a treat to hear him say that, to exhibit the grace I had long known in his father, Bill Hollins.

Publications Span Races

Journalism and the world of student publications, like athletics and organizations, is fertile ground for growing a team spirit and camaraderie that lets race, like different hair color and different family background, be simply another aspect, not a dominating factor, of the person.

Newspaper journalism and yearbook journalism were two different classes, but the groups shared everything from a classroom and office area and cameras to bus seats and hotel rooms on our trips to press conventions, workshops, and interscholastic competitions. A few students were in both groups.

Each course was taught as if all students were going into professional newspaper or magazine work. Even with routine lessons from textbooks, class activity revolved around the respective publication. Deadlines varied to fit the three-week newspaper cycle and contract deadlines in the twelve-month cycle of the yearbook, a news magazine of the year.

I was disappointed that so few blacks were interested in publications work, but those we had were memorable for their ingenuity, congeniality, and reliability, not to mention an original sense of humor. Several still stand out for me.

Thomas Morris was on the yearbook staff soon after integration, and his division page drawings are memorable still in the 1968 yearbook. He used an overhead projector for the outlines but literally redrew each photograph with an ink pen.

Argie Hollins, sports editor after the usual one-year stint as a reporter, threw himself into editing with full force. His only participant sport was basketball, but he was heartily involved as a spectator/booster in all sports. He could be heard at nearly every contest, enthusiastically urging on the Cranes.

He could be a clown too.

Both staffs attended summer workshops at Texas Tech. During the photo workshop, Argie would not let Ricky Leaman, his roommate, refer to *color* film.

"Please," he said, stiffening his lean six-foot frame, "say *black*."

Argie had a beautiful, deep bass voice heard often in school assemblies, so we asked him to represent us in the talent show on the first evening of an Interscholastic League Press Conference Convention in Austin. He couldn't decide—or wouldn't tell—what he would sing, but when he walked his long, lean frame onto the stage wearing boots, a toy pistol, and ten-gallon hat, his "Tall, Dark Stranger" literally brought down the house.

Outgoing editors participated with me—and usually made the final decisions—in the selection of the following year's editors, chosen from among the first-year students. Argie was outvoted in part of the decision. So he got to us in a "farewell high-jink."

One strict rule was about not using cutesy items and nonsensical phrases to fill out the newspaper pages. If copy ran a little short, the page editor was to insert one of the short items he was supposed to keep on hand. But when the final issue of the *Crane* came out, there it was: *Happy Summer,* in bold type, spaced out to fill a two-inch by two-column space. I scolded, of course, but naught was to be done about it, and Argie had been too good an editor to penalize his grade for such stuff. So I allowed him his moment of insanity and the last word. Louie later told me Argie's layout disobedience was his retaliation to the other editors and me for not letting him have his way in the selection of *all* the new editors.

Louie too was a mainstay of enthusiasm and reliability. He was a vital part of the publications team, competing with, as well as urging on, his fellow editors, standing for thoroughness and sensitive objectivity in everything he did. His sense of humor too was notable. Nowhere else have I seen more evidence that among young people, color was just another aspect of personality, neither to be ignored nor made a big deal of. Sometimes it provided material for humor.

Louie and Cheryl Fox, a white girl who would follow Louie as sports editor the next year, were talking during a Coke break at a practice UIL meet. Cheryl was drinking coffee.

"Didn't your parents tell you what that would do to you?" Louie asked, and Cheryl responded, "Oh, is that what happened to you, Louie?"

Those two plus Mike McKay, white and editor-in-chief, became a threesome on many projects, joking as they worked seriously, and vice versa. They later carried that friendship into college journalism at Angelo State University and came together to meet our group a couple of times when we went to the ILPC convention in Austin.

Gina Vaughn was in journalism only her senior year, so was never an editor, but she was an enthusiastic reporter, always "on the team." Just recently she told again what fun she'd had and how much she'd learned. No surprise—she would have fun and learn wherever she went.

Technicalities

Skin color was a technical factor in one aspect of publications work: photography. It happened first in group team pictures, all done by student photographers who had been taught to put taller people on the back row. Well, guess what—black athletes were nearly all tallest on the team. So the indiscriminate flash whitened out the front row and—especially if the photo was taken in the middle of the gym, with no close wall background—blended the darker skins back into the dark surroundings, with almost comical results.

Our student photographers, who also did their own darkroom work then, could improve on the situation somewhat with skillful hand blocking of light from the enlarger, but that took extra time and was only barely satisfactory. Hence a new rule: sitting or kneeling, black people go on the front row.

Almost always there was good humor in these situations. Something we figured out together.

Camaraderie, and sometimes revelations, continued after graduation. When kids get away from school on an extracurricular trip, they almost forget—or don't care—that a teacher is around, as they horseplay and compare notes and memories. Ask any teacher. Likewise when former students visit casually after graduation.

On one trip, several journalism students present and past were talking about antics in classes, what they got away with and what they didn't.

Louie said he had been discriminated against: some band members would sneak at random times behind the stage curtain and eat a snack or two. ("I was a drummer, not a horn blower, so it wasn't that bad.") But he was the one who always got caught. Fine friends his white comrades turned out to be, he said. They kept giving him powdered, sugarcoated Twinkies.

"No one told me I had that white on my face," he said, "until the band director easily saw it."

Another way the black students had fun with color happened when our traveling group would go into a restaurant together. Someone would start calling me "Mom," and pretty soon there were several all claiming to be mine, but no one said it more loudly and plainly in front of the waiters than Louie and Argie—and then they laughed at the odd stares.

Mom I felt like sometimes—whether or not I had any of my own children with me—and always my heart went out to black moms and the heartache they must have felt through the years when their children were slighted only because of skin color. But those parents were some of the wisest, enduring such indignities and still preparing their children with grace against the day those children might have it better. Ordinary people, possessing character with a capital C and processing that character before and with their children.

---

27 Will Allen Dromgoole, "The Bridge Builder," in *Father: An Anthology of Verse* (E. P. Dutton & Company, 1931).

28 Clifton Fadiman, *Huckleberry Finn by Mark Twain*, Encyclopedia Britannica Films, Inc. (Chicago, IL: Encyclopedia Britannica films, 1965).

READER'S NOTES

Grace under Pressure
Ernest Hemingway's definition of guts in *A Farewell to Arms*

And thou shalt number seven Sabbaths of years, unto thee, seven times seven years; and the space of seven sabbaths of years shall be unto thee forty and nine years.

Then shalt thou cause the trumpet of the jubilee to sound on the tenth day of the seventh month, on the day of atonement shall ye make the trumpet sound throughout all your land.

And ye shall hallow the fiftieth year, and proclaim liberty throughout the land to all the inhabitants thereof: it shall be a jubilee unto you; and ye shall return every man unto his possession, and ye shall return every man unto his family.

—Leviticus 25:8–10, 13 KJV

Chapter 6

GRACE UNDER PRESSURE, FAITH OVER ALL

Call this stereotyping on my part, but no one masters that art of Hemingway's like the black folks I know.

Their cscrimination, was to be very deferential and courteous toward whites. But I don't believe that's the only reason that when the light at the end of their tunnel began to brighten and then finally shone on nearly all their rights, they were more appreciative of getting those God-given and constitutionally-given rights than they were bitter about having had to wait so long. Appreciation seems inbred.

Ellis and Company

The not-just-tolerant but kindly and reasonable side of grace was in Ellis Lane's demeanor when Sue Christon came to him with an urgency to prove, among other things, that her daddy had not built that wall for reasons of hate. Ellis did find documents to show official reasons for the wall.

Perhaps a best personification of grace surfaced in the wake of a sad, disappointing crime. On a cool afternoon during the Christmas holidays in 2010, the building occupied by the Faith in Christ Baptist Church, the same building previously occupied by the First Baptist Church, on the site of the original black population "squatter" settlement in the thirties and forties, went up in flames.

An arsonist, who also started three other flames in Crane—most at church- or religion-related buildings—that same day, somehow had the whole south part of the rambling building, the part that housed oak pews and pulpit furniture, fully aflame before someone alerted firemen. There were tears aplenty as blacks and whites alike stood at the site and reminisced of good times and meaningful experiences within the sixty-year-old structure. And sad words aplenty on the Crane e-mail exchange before dark that day, as the word went out long before the flames did.

My family had our own memories and grief that Christmas. When we moved to Crane in 1955, the sanctuary and west wing had already been built with volunteer labor, and we were just in time to help with the north wing and the chapel, extreme northeast corner. I say we, but this was the fifties, and men did most of the hammer-and-nails part of building while the women mostly gave support help, sandwiches and coffee and the like, to the builders. We built something else—friendships that would outlast the century—on the roof of that chapel.

A generation later, both our daughters had been married there, and subsequently their children started Sunday school in the nursery that was now a charred, wet ruin. When FBC bought land and erected a new building on the south end of Crane, disposing of the building at Fourth and Sue Streets seemed a problem until someone found that the Faith in Christ congregation would take the building just as it was, operate in the sound part, and apply patience and time to working on the other parts.

That's grace.

Because the "rock" walls—homemade bricks—were wobbly after the wood was burned away, the local fire department razed them for safety's sake. On New Year's Day I finally saw the rubble for the first time, and the nostalgia was predictable. The tears didn't last long, though, as Ellis toured the building remainder with us, pointing out the good that was left.

"It could have been a lot worse," he said, noting they still had the part of the building they used. The kitchen and Fellowship Hall, both part of the chapel wing, were not even smoke damaged.

We moved west through the Sunday school hall, the corridors in a square that had seemed miles long to many a child, black, brown, and white, until we came to the start of the block-long hall on the west end, leading to the sanctuary, the first structure of the forties.

Two rooms had been readapted for today's needs. One in which I had once attended my adult Sunday school class was now a clothes closet, where neat racks held donated clothing ready for folks in need. Another near a small bathroom, had been outfitted with two beds for visiting preachers or others who needed shelter for a night or so.

Seeing that led to a discussion of the day when churches were never locked, when they could serve as a spiritual and even physical sanctuary to nearly anyone who deemed he needed it. It was once well known among local church members that transients had stopped over in their buildings. There was no trashing or damage, just an occasional sandwich wrapper or discarded newspaper found by whoever came into the building first the next day.

When we stopped at that impossible pile of burnt rafters and broken stone at the entrance to the long west hall, the carpet squishing under our feet, Ellis praised the Crane Volunteer Fire Department and help from neighboring towns for their wisdom in attacking that juncture first to make a watery gap to prevent the fire from moving over the north wing and the chapel.

"I need to be vacuuming this water up," he said, "but we don't have our electricity back yet." That's the old-school pastor, who feels obliged to care for the physical as well as the spiritual premises.

A practical as well as sentimental grief was shared by us all: two dozen or more long, solid oak pews, each a treasure in itself, lost to fire. There had been other, shorter pews, on each side of the auditorium, and several church members had purchased these. My husband and I had bought a couple for grown daughters, who had squirmed many an hour on those same seats.

"Lots a people had tried to buy those pews, but we would not sell them," Ellis said. I mused aloud about how much antique dealers might have given for them, money to help materialize the dreams of making a gym or the like in the area. But Ellis turned us to the positive.

The FIC congregation had used only the northernmost wing and the chapel. Ellis explained that they had looked into getting insurance earlier but simply couldn't afford it.

"Since all parts were connected, we would have had to insure the whole building by the square foot," he said, "and we just couldn't.

"So we had to do without insurance. We had talked about separating the wings, taking a section out, so as to insure the part we use. But we invited the Lord to the business meeting that night. It was all in his plans, and now we can get insurance and do other things to protect our building."

We shared rueful smiles and maybe shed another tear as we walked outside into the courtyard, scene of many a dinner on the grounds, many a Sunday school and vacation Bible school playtime. There had been no damage to the fledgling trees planted by FIC congregation or the latticed brick fence the FIC congregation had built.

The fire department had retrieved the cornerstone, and we talked about whether it should be saved on site or moved to the present-day FBC building. I leaned toward the former, with perhaps an addendum stone noting the FIC's occupation of the structure. But it wasn't up to me, and what counts is that the congregation and volunteer firemen had thought to salvage the stone before removing the debris.

Nostalgia's not a bad thing, maybe even a little cathartic, as we look at the "good ole days" with love, while noting that these are "good new days," in part because of forebears whose labor bore fruit for us. I could do it that New Year's Day as I found myself uplifted by a man who represented folks who rely upon the supreme Actor of Grace.

The arsonist's forgiveness was a given, not to be modified with explanations. What is forgiveness but passing on the grace such the forgivers have themselves received? It is mercy and other such attributes as godly people see coming from above.

"Our concern and our prayer are for him to get Lord's forgiveness."

I know he meant that. In days when blacks were not welcome in white churches, white visitors to black congregations were greeted without question, with smiles and open arms. When black teachers were not welcome in white schools, Bethune loved having white visitors at their basketball games, and black teachers appreciated help from white teachers with setting up some science equipment and the like, which we had "handed down" to them.

When black folks had to sit at the back of the bus and chivalry was supposedly in fashion, I as a young woman in Corpus Christi had a black man rise and offer me his seat in the marginal part of the colored section. I smiled inside at the looks from white men who had not offered theirs.

It's the same forgiving, gracious faith that must have strengthened their endurance during years of slavery, years of discrimination. Surely they wondered why the Lord was so long in freeing them, while "Let my people go" was their relentless prayer. Parents then and now made do, insisted as far as they could on education, and taught their children how to get along against the day when more opportunities would come.

Essentially they had to forgive the great masses of us who were born into the system, felt a vague uneasiness about it, but did nothing—sinned by omission—until more courageous folks brought about some action.

Faith in Georgia

But their anchor of faith seems universal with folks like Ellis and his congregation and his neighbors. One example appears in Melissa Faye Green's *Praying for Sheetrock*, her nonfiction story of the 1970s political awakening in a little black village and a white community on the Georgia coast.

She said that their faith was their life, and—especially the older generation—they never doubted the consistency of faith would pay off, eventually.

> If the Messiah did arrive today, the old black people of McIntosh would be the least astonished group in America. They might send a young person to go and look, and those with telephones might call their daughters, but the rest would remain in their upholstered rockers with their quilts across their laps, and finish their coffee. And wait to be called upon personally.
>
> [They] have lived in close, practical, and well-understood terms with God all their lives. If a messenger of God were to appear on their porch one morning, there'd be no awkwardness of address, no groping for greetings of sufficient splendor, no fumbling for religious rituals as exercised in childhood, and no exaggerated prostration, either: "Gertie, angel of the Lord's here!"
>
> God may work in subtle or even inscrutable ways. What people sow, in due time they are likely to reap.

If they pay attention, the world glitters with God's lessons all around them. And when in the 1970s the white people invoked history, the black people, packing their churches, called out to God.

So it has been in the Southwest. Via their faith, many black folks have transcended circumstances, as their forebears did for generations.

God is good, as Greene said, and where others may see coincidence, these see and express the hand of God. The hope may have seemed ephemeral at times, but it had substance enough to cling to.[29]

Jubilee Restored

There was no coincidence, according to Billy Joe Neal and others, in the timing of the transfer of the First Baptist Church building to the Faith in Christ congregation. It was on the site of the black settlement early in Crane's history.

The actual conversation in which he advanced this belief needs repeating here, as it shows more emotion and confidence than I could convey by paraphrase.

He and I were talking with his wife, Inola Hollins Neal, and Sue Neeley Christon when Billy led into his thinking.

"You know," he said, "in the Bible where it speaks the peace of jubilee. The fiftieth year—did you know that?"

"Oh yes," I said, "seven times seven years, and then it would be forty-nine and then the—"

"But you know what happened then?"

"They returned to their ancestral land?"

"Um-hum," he said, "and look who's in that church now—fifty years almost to the day after they were asked to leave their squatters' camp. Another guy pointed that out to me."

Sue, who had been brokenhearted when the FBC congregation built a new structure and left the one she had watched her daddy and others labor on, finally entered this conversation.

"Oh praise God," she said. "I'm glad somebody's using it. Daddy would be thrilled to death." She turned to me.

"You've been asking me hard questions. Let me ask you one—why did they want to go build a new church building out on the hill, anyway?" I began to explain what I knew of the technical and logistic considerations, but Billy Joe returned to his view.

"But see I want to tell you something about that," he said. "Sometimes we don't even know why we do certain things, but the First Baptist got an itch they couldn't scratch—they had to get a new building. I consider it divine intervention that caused them to do this—fifty years from 1947, when the blacks were moved from that site."

He also mentioned that the arrangement with the Faith in Christ congregation was negotiated by the FBC pastor at that time, whose name was—David Miracle.

Another symbol? Providential? Bill thinks so.

In the forties, Sue had been still taking nearly every step her Daddy took around town and on his building projects, and she remembered helping with the homemade concrete blocks for the outside of the building.

"The men had dug a pond in the ground to mix the concrete, and built forms," she said. "Then they put some speckled coloring in the concrete, and we scooped the concrete into those forms to dry."

Most of the first part of the building—the sanctuary at Fourth and Sue Streets—was done with volunteer labor. Sue and Gene, her older, half brother, had given that auditorium its first coat of paint, "'Cause Daddy was busy on other things."

Volunteers were church members and perhaps a few nonmember associates. But Billy remembered hearing about some black men who were hired—for seventy-five cents a day—to work on the construction.

"One guy was telling me about that, and he said Earnest Hollins said he wasn't gonna work for those wages, but they gave him a couple weeks, and there he was."

We talked for a few minutes about the FBC decision to construct a new building instead of renovating the old one. Billy said he knew there were many handicaps in renovating or rebuilding a structure of that size, but no matter, as the whole shift was engineered providentially.

So there we have it: the black squatters' camp had been moved in 1947, and half a century later, after talking about the building decision for ten years under three pastors, the congregation constructed and moved into a new structure. The old building was sold for a nominal fee to the Faith in Christ group.

The symbols go on: FIC's pastor, Ellis Lane, was in the first integrated class to graduate from Crane High School; Ellis and Sue were the first ones of our day to look up the facts about the black population movement and the wall; and Faith in Christ group is not exclusively black but integrated.

Bucilla

Long before anyone started rocking the segregation boat, Bucilla Abron showed some ladylike—that's a deliberate and exact term— qualities of kindness and love to folks around here. In my early, circa 1960, days of teaching in Crane, I required substitutes at home. Though it was a strain on the budget, there was a time when I had both a babysitter—an elderly lady who could not do heavy housework—and also a housecleaner. One day a week, Mrs. Effie Gray and Mrs. Bucilla Abron [later Bowens] enjoyed each other's company while they did their jobs. Bucilla endeared herself to our children too.

They're grown, and she's old—like me—but they still love her as much as they did Mrs. Gray. After school some days, Mrs. Gray would stay and chat a while, and often she told of their good conversations and the sweet attitude toward life she saw in Bucilla.

"Bucilla told me what a great time she had with her girls," Gray said one day, "picking up pecans around the courthouse and then shelling them and making pies. She shows me how to enjoy every little thing in life."

Dorothy Abron Brown said recently how it had hurt that, while she had to call other adults Mr./Mrs. and last name, white children could call her mom by the first name. But that's the way we were, and somehow it would now seem an affectation for me to say "Mrs. Bowens." I think she knows I love and respect her as much as any "Mrs."

Even after we were doing better racially hereabouts, folks like Bucilla were still—although a little more subtly—at the mercy of white folks. One night after an automobile fender-bender, she told me that officials had matter-of-factly sent her car to a repair shop not of her choosing.

"I just don't think that was right," she said, and I agreed, but tacitly we both knew we didn't want the hassle of following up on that—I for my own convenience but she to keep from disturbing someone's peace and probably still losing the battle with residual racists in high places. The grace came not from the high places but from a gentle black woman still deferential in "keeping her place"—and the peace.

Daisy

Daisy Jeffery was Daisy Lane when I first knew her. She was one of the former Bethune basketball girls who added much appreciated experience to our CHS newly starting girls' teams. Because I had daughters on the team, I sometimes helped transport the girls and never saw or heard anything among them to suggest that black and white young people didn't fit to their new situation with gracious congeniality and adaptability.

So I wasn't surprised at Daisy's reaction years later when she had such a time getting a teaching position in the Crane schools. She had worked for years as a special education aide, putting in the same hours as the certified teachers, while she also completed her college degree, mothered several young people besides her own children in her and husband Jackie's family, was a helpmate to Jackie in his duties as pastor, and kept up her interest in and attendance at athletic contests.

Having taught just down the hall from Daisy, visited in her classroom, and watched her conduct with students and staff, I had hoped everyone, including her supervisors, could have seen what she was and hired her as a teacher as soon as she was certified. Not so. During those years of applying several different places, she was offered a job at a neighboring town and then had to weigh the expense and, especially, time away from home that job would cost. She opted to continue as an aide for Crane until, in the fall of 2006, she was employed as a teacher. What a pleasure it was for me to be back on the school board just in time to vote to employ Daisy.

W. T. Wright

A professional insult must be extremely difficult to respond to graciously, but Dr. W. T. Wright would know. When integration of schools was legally unavoidable, so was the need to employ a quota of the professional staff from Bethune in the integrated school. Though one official had been heard to say there would "never be a N---- [sic]" teaching in his school, a sidewise solution barely conformed to the law while depriving some students of a highly qualified teacher/administrator.

Bethune principal Dr. Wright, one of the most highly educated teachers in the system (with an earned doctorate), an ordained minister of a sizeable church in Odessa, was made audio-visual coordinator in Crane Elementary—a task held previously by an aide.

Wright is gone now, but his wife, Winnie, said recently that, while W. T. had contemplated moving to another school where he was offered a job, he decided to stay for notable reasons.

"We wanted all three children to graduate here," she said in the same firm but soft voice I'd heard her use as a Crane Hospital nurse. "It was a good system."[30]

Also, the job put W. T. in the same building as their younger children, as well as other black children adjusting to the change. Another wise and thoughtful motive.

I witnessed a scene when Dr. Wright calmly handled a near-scuffle among young people black and white, showing his very reason for taking this insult of a position. He chose, I am sure, to help not only "his people," as whites often blandly called them, but all young people through these times of adjustment. Grace didn't yield to pressure.

Winnie told that W. T. had an office shared with a janitor. She also told that the elementary principal was "so angry" that Wright was put in such a job that he—the principal—left soon after that.

So what happened to the other teachers from Bethune? No one seems to remember the details, but they faded away, certainly quietly and I'm guessing gracefully.

Other examples of ungracious treatment are rife, even after integration, usually involving certain individuals clinging to some old ways of thinking, but most were handled, or tolerated, with grace.

Likewise their attitude toward personal tragedies not of their making. Such as when a loved one dies before the parent, but she is grateful for a peaceful death and talks of the "big, big party" they're going to have when she gets to heaven.

Death, Where Is Thy Sting?

So it was and is in many black communities, including Crane's Bethune community. Death is dealt with as providential, a step in existence for one on personal terms with God. When Bucilla Abron lost her daughter Patsy, she eagerly told at the funeral that Patsy had said, early that day, she was going on a trip.

"I asked her where, and she said, 'I can't tell you because you won't want me to go now, but it will be all right.' Then that afternoon when she died outside, she was lying straight on her back, settled down with feet pointed upward."

No doubt to Bucilla and family that Patsy had known what trip she was going to take.

Yes, these folks see God's work all around and rely on Him for the ultimate good. No wonder they were graceful about forgiving and accepting their white friends when integration came.

Of course our being a young town helped. There was no local heritage of slavery, no background of "that black boy's great-grandfather used to be my family's slave," such as I heard in Mississippi and Louisiana small towns in the sixties. Or, "That old black man is a cousin of our neighbor, Ms. ---. See how light he is?"

In Crane, there were no such generational memories but a camaraderie of sorts among people who—or whose immediate ancestors—came to the oil field because there was more money, or maybe just money, period, to be made. That included not only Depression-ridden white families who were happy to have a job but also black "servant class" grateful to get a few cents more per hour.

So that was part of the kinship—we're nearly all better off here than where we came from, and we have always known it.

More Glimpses of Grace

Faith often brought kinships closer. When First Baptist Church held the dedication of their new building a decade or so ago, Pastor Jackie Jeffery of Mount Zion Church attended and spoke of the closeness between the two congregations, of how FBC had helped Mount Zion, and how many other congregations had supported the only black church here in those early days.

Yes, there were folks who turned up their noses or mumbled discouragement at the first blacks who dared visit white churches. Pastor Jeffery, if he even thought of that anymore, graciously ignored it.

Here we must exclude the Crane Church of Christ from that indictment, as they had blacks in their congregation in the fifties, notably Billy Van Jones and his grandmother.

Soon after FBC constructed a new building came the problem of what to do with the abandoned building, to put it to best use. There was a new, independent congregation hereabouts, mostly though not completely black, called the Faith in Christ Church. They didn't need such a large facility, of course—neither had FBC in recent years—but were happy to get a "fixer-upper." They went to work immediately "fixing it up," to use phrasing Texans understand.

This then became the FIC Baptist Church and affiliated with the Southern Baptist Convention. That didn't mean they gave up any independence, just aligned more officially to cooperate with fellow Christians who shared the basic beliefs about salvation and missions.

And with the burning tragedy came more visible love from the community. Accounts were set up for contributions to FIC in both local banks and began to fill immediately as announcements were made in church congregations, Lions Club, Senior Citizens, and other groups throughout the town and county.

The First United Methodist Church made their building available for the FIC group until their own building could be usable again. Methodists also sponsored a fundraising lunch, conveniently at a Sunday-after-church time. Most folks of course paid more than the seven dollars a plate being charged for chicken-fried steak and all the trimmings Texans expect with that. Members of nearly every church in town were not only attending but cooking, serving, and the like.

That's where Ellis said another prayer had been answered and that the perpetrator of the crime had come to know the Lord.

"That," he said, "makes it all worthwhile."

Folks around him, black and white, nodded.

Then he said that replacing/repairing the electrical wiring was not going to be as expensive as they had thought, and now insurance would be within reason.

"God don't make no mistakes," he said.

"Ol' devil's still at work, but he's not gonna win."

And More

Some examples have been told in earlier chapters, such as the high school senior who was denied the valedictorian's position because he had not been in CHS two years. Some will be told later, such as the teenager who faced the city and county leadership for justice in the swimming pool situation, and the athlete who coolly played his great ball with never a nod for racial slurs on the sidelines.

Many blacks, who remain nameless here, knew they did "have it good," *relatively*. That is, they had the grace to appreciate the good and to endure the not-so-good while waiting for a better day.

I daresay few blacks in Texas had higher-paying jobs than the teachers at Bethune School, not to credit Crane's indulgence: our pay was among the highest in the state, so to keep the separate but equal mode—at least on official paperwork—black and white teachers were on the same pay scale.

Just one of the factors bringing some young folks back home to the place they had been glad to get out of.

---

29 Melissa Faye Green *Praying for Sheetrock*. Reading, Massachusetts: Addison-Wesley Publishig, Inc.
30 Winnie Wright, telephone interview.

READER'S NOTE

One's home is the safest refuge.
—Sir Edmund Clark[31]

Chapter 7

YOU CAN GO HOME AGAIN

S<small>AFETY, PEACE AND QUIET, AND ANCESTRAL</small> connections are reasons some Crane blacks, like their counterparts throughout America, come home.

Some black citizens who are still here—and others here again—say that when they were growing up "behind the wall" they felt safe, and lessons learned there taught them to be shrewd and careful and generous and deferential about their behavior, especially when venturing beyond that safety.

Now that they can venture out at will—or even to live—they "know who the racists are" and so generally avoid them. That measure of safety is perhaps the reason some have returned who had earlier intended to wipe our dust off their feet forever.

When blacks come home to a particular town, like Crane, or home to the South generally or specifically, they don't find things all rosy but mostly know how to deal with the glitches: racism as well as opportunity, past hurts as well as old and new friendships. So do some of the whites they come home to.

Home to Crane

Crane seems a kind of microcosm for this movement "home" for blacks. It may be for a job opportunity, or to get their children out of the big cities and back to the place where parents can keep up with them, or to get their sea legs for a career, or to care for an aging parent, or maybe just to rest and recuperate and find their lives again.

Coming back for Crane blacks is not always pretty, but one beautiful thing about it for people like me is the discovery and development of some wonderful relationships and seeing some talents we might have missed under the old segregation rule.

Dorothy: Led by Higher Power

In spite of earlier resolutions never to live in Crane again, Dorothy Abron Brown did come back some thirty years after she left. After a personal upheaval, a divorce she was not ready for, she turned her thoughts westward. Something kept leading her that way—to return to Crane, live with her mother and let her son attend Crane High School, and—she dared to think of fulfilling a longtime dream: attend college.

> We were married for twenty-nine years—he was my first love, I always loved my husband, and I thought we'd be there forever. So I kept praying, asking God, "Should I stay here or should I move? It's on You. You've got to show me what I need to do."
>
> Mind you, I always told myself I'd never go back, I'd never live in Crane again because I didn't have any fond memories there—but never say *never*.
>
> But I kept praying, and I received my answer and still said, "Lord, You sure you want me to go?" I always do a test like the fleece—let it be wet all around the fleece, let just the fleece be wet, you know, and I kept trying God, "Okay, are you sure you want me to go? Are you sure this is what you want me to do?"
>
> And my answer kept coming back the same, so I loaded up everything I own, and we moved to Crane,

my son and I. My daughter was already married and gone, so my son and I came. I told my family I moved down here on God's word, so I'm just crazy enough to believe that He's gonna keep me.

He has kept me—helped me too. I did remodeling on a house, electrical work, all kinds of things. I even dug my sewer and put in new lines—a lot of things, with God giving me the strength. He blocks the blows, you know."

But the dream of college was harder to materialize.

When I graduated from Crane High School, a note on my transcript said, "Not recommended for college." You think that's not a terrible thing? Every time I saw that, it did something to me. It killed my spirit, and it still bothers me. When I went to Houston after high school, I was going to go to college, and I called Crane and had them send my transcript, and again I saw that—I didn't go.

So here I was in 2000, back in Crane at age forty-nine. I even signed up for school and everything, and when I reread that transcript, I stayed out another two years. But I kept praying, "Okay, God, I moved down here because You led me."

So I decided, okay, I'm going to go to college because of something in my spirit. So I said, "Okay, God, You have to help me with the grades, with the school, just help me. This is on You." I entered Odessa College, and I prayed for strength, and I was successful. Because I had no college credit, I had to start from the bottom and work my way through, but the second semester I was on the dean's list. I was secretary of student government; I even experienced college dorm life. I went on field trips and was involved in everything any normal-age freshman college student would be involved in. It was the greatest experience, and I thank God for it.

Odessa College, yes, ma'am—the greatest years of my life. I knew all my instructors, and I met with them and I told them, "I'm here to get an education and that's it." My favorite instructor was Wayne Johnson. We fought just like Mr. Lilly and me at Bethune. He taught writing slash literature, not literature, writing slash English. He would critique my papers. He was so tough, and I told him, I said, "You can do all you want to; I'm not leaving. You're stuck with me."

But we became the best of friends, and he made me a better person, you know. He said, "Dorothy, when you're talking to me, you talk with your everyday common voice, but when you're talking to the other instructors, you need to use your college voice and use what you've learned." So he had to stay on me to do that.

I didn't have time for other things. I couldn't go off on weekends, because I do anything, I have to do my best, even if it kills me. My sister would come to visit, and she said, "Well, you don't have to study tonight. You don't have to do this." But if I took off an hour, that would mean an extra hour or two that I had to stay up later at night. At OC, I stayed in the library. They had couches and teased me, saying, "Dorothy stays here so much we got couches so she can take a nap and then get back to studying."

But I'd have to have peace and quiet because I'm old-school and can't have music and noise and all of that. I have to keep reading and reading to get an understanding. I got an associate of arts degree, and I know nobody but God allowed it.

> After I finished there, I wanted to go on and take [more] college credit, but I was kind of scared to take the challenge. Now I've gotten rusty. But I wanted to let Crane know, I think it should not be put on the transcript, "Not recommended for college." You don't know who can do what.

Dorothy could not say her son's CHS experience was the best.

> It was pretty much the same as mine had been. Before we came, I had two sisters tell coaches we were moving down and my son was an excellent football player—he played a little basketball, but football was his thing. And the coach said, "Just move him down, just come on down, and we'll work with him, and we'll work and—" It didn't happen that way. It seemed like a personality conflict or whatever. My son wasn't given much opportunity to play.
>
> When I was in high school, the coach prevented me from playing volleyball. I loved volleyball. I was a tomboy, I'm good at my serve, I was a good player, but the coach had already picked out who was gonna play. I would keep going to practice, working out with the other girls, running laps with the girls, doing everything all the other girls were doing.
>
> Freshman, sophomore, junior, senior—every year I tried out, and I stayed just about until the last game. Sometimes my nails would be so split because we used to have to hit balls, but I kept practicing, I kept running. But I never made the team. I am a hard worker but was never given the opportunity, and I resented that.
>
> After I came back, I did Census 2000 and went to that coach's house. I was working for the state, so I didn't get involved or ask her any extra questions.

I said, "Hello, do you know me?" She said, "Yes, Dorothy, I know you."

But I couldn't get out of character. I didn't want her to file anything against the state because I was out of line.

My sister Joyce holds a record for basketball, but she didn't play volleyball. But I was interested in volleyball. Carol, she wasn't sports oriented, but she went with the girls and helped with their towels and whatever. What do they call that? Trainer.

Two blacks, Janet and Daisy Lane, played. I don't know if it was my spirit. I don't know if it was—she's gone today, and I'll never know.

Nicole: A Pro Early On

Gradually the situation was better for Crane returnees. After retirement, I did some substitute teaching, and what an eye-opener that was—would have been for any old teacher. A substitute can tell a great deal about the regular teacher. Lesson plans and directions left for the sub, look of the room, and especially behavior of students—all are signs, subtle or billboard size, about what kind of teacher this is.

Imagine my delight when I substituted for Nicole Jeffery, whose parents were among that first wave of Bethune students when we integrated, and discovered she was a good teacher. In her early years of teaching, she was clearly what I like to call a real pro, whose students felt free to ask questions and to laugh, and—I felt good about this English class. I was glad Nicole "came home again," though to this point she had left only for college. I'm glad she wanted to get her first teaching experience—and was allowed to—in this place where she had begun her own good education.

Later she taught in an inner-city school in Fort Worth and found herself in a whole new world, realizing just how protected she had felt in Crane. She wrote in an e-mail of those times.

Sometimes it feels as if I am a character in someone's novel, about the small town, sheltered girl who moves to the big city to deal with the problems of inner city children while trying to teach them, through literature, that there is a better life outside of Stop Six, Eastwood, and Poly [Polytechnic School]. So just one generation removed from segregation, she seemed to be an illustration of integration's success.

As of August 2014, Nicole is principal of Crane Elementary School. She was a principal elsewhere when she interviewed with Superintendent Jim Rummage. She told him she had been waiting for this opportunity for several years.

"I had already told my mom and dad [Jackie and Daisy Lane Jeffery] I would move one more time—if I had the chance to come back to Crane—and never intended to move again."

Talk about coming home. And her twin girls love it too. After all, in Fort Worth they had only lawns to play on, but here they have plenty of good dirt and sand for mud pies and the like.

Others

Many interviewed here have left Crane, not only for college but for other work experience, and returned for varied reasons.

Jo Ann Davenport Littleton came some years back to be close to her mother, Irene Drones, but lived in Odessa for work reasons, saying she would never leave the area while her mother was alive. Irene spent her last years in her own little suite at Jo Ann's house in Odessa, with Jo Ann's half brother Cedric Drones. She is gone now, but Jo Ann's still there, most of the time. Her husband's business is in the Metroplex, and they do much commuting between two homes.

Cookie, Daisy, Janet, Johnnie, Ellis, Carolyn, Blondie—many of the Lane children are back in Crane or Odessa, and they nearly all show up for special events like reunions.

Likewise the Abron and Bowens families.

And Neals. And Jefferys.

Louie Jones, a Lane cousin, returned to live after developing near-debilitating illness and retiring from his work at Texas Tech in Lubbock.

Yet another disclaimer: this work (STI) features accomplishments and forward movements in integration and improving compatibilities between the races but is not meant to give the impression that everything was or is sweetness and light.

The hope is that accenting the positive will bring more positives, but some lingering negatives must be acknowledged. Most returnees are, like Dorothy, sure God had led them back, but still they face negatives. So do others who go home again in other places.

Home to the South

The southward return of blacks is not unique to Crane, or even to Texas. It's happening, sometimes surprisingly, throughout the South, and for reasons not so surprising, considering human nature of any color.

"It's all about quality of life," said one retiree from New York to Palm Court, Florida, quoted by Larry Copeland in a *USA Today* article.[32]

"When I return to New York, it's culture shock," said the interviewee. "I don't hear car horns down here; as soon as you get to New York, you're hearing thousands of them."

Copeland told of the major demographic shift documented in the last census: blacks are moving from Northeastern and Midwestern cities to cities and suburbs of the South, not all retirees.

"They are drawn," Copeland said, "by the lure of jobs, by the prospect of making their money go further, by the warm climate and other amenities, and by family ties. In some cases they feel a cultural pull to the region their ancestors left decades ago."

He quotes sociology professor Silas Lee of New Orleans in saying that the South really is the family roots for the majority of African Americans anywhere in the country.

Magazine publisher J. Kevin Powell of Atlanta, formerly of Maryland, said there is a piece of him that is southern, "that thing of speaking to everybody I see."

Morgan Freeman: Peace and Solitude and Safety

Notable blacks like Morgan Freeman even left Hollywood (as a residence, not as a workplace) to go to—yes, their personal places of safety.[33] Half a century after he left Mississippi, never imagining he would ever want to return, Freeman did just that. He moved back to spend time with his mother, who was growing older, living in the house that had been her parents' in Charleston. Then he bought adjacent land to build his own home next door.

He lives on land worked by his ancestors, and now his mother is buried near her modest home. It's a reminder of where he came from—*from* being the operative word here.

Writer Nancy Griffin, writing for AARP magazine, quoted him: "You know, you can go around the world, and you have eaten and stayed in the best hotels. But here there is peace and quiet and solitude. And the realization that this has always represented safety.

"Psychic safety. So I tell people I'm where I'm supposed to be."

So Morgan has come full circle—not in the sense of finishing and tying up the past but more like forming a past-to-present-to-future chain link.

Regarding the residues of racism, Griffin told that Morgan, like Bill Cosby, has long encouraged people of color to take responsibility for their lives. In that tone, he said he doesn't downplay race.

"I just don't play it," he said, and once told *Sixty Minutes*' Mike Wallace that the best way to deal with racism is just to quit talking about it.

Generally that's where we in Crane are getting also. In West Texas we see the under-twenty-fives becoming tired of the subject, and the transitional generation (those who started school at Bethune and finished at integrated Crane High School) are becoming increasingly ready to move beyond the subject. Luckily for me in rounding out this work, a few of my former students and their parents are willing to talk about it, maybe just in deference to me?

Those uninterested black young people are generally of the generation who never attended a segregated school or swam in a segregated pool, or entered a house through the back door or rode at the back of a bus, those long-ago situations. All the more reason to get written records straight for them, against the day when they may want to know the whole truth, the real history.

And a certain amount of talking is therapeutic. As we give each other tacit permission to deal unabashedly with topics we would once have steered clear of, we find out how alike we are as people, quite apart from societal categorizing.

Society's walls and lines, visible or not, have made for an estrangement we may never get over as a whole people, and surely not in my lifetime. But we all have a part to do to get past that stuff. We must.

As we come to terms with the facts of segregation, we realize it was much worse and also better on personal levels than even many who lived the time could see then. My dear friend and former student Louie Jones said to tell much more about it would be too painful; Louie's uncle, Jack Lane, made it clear when I first interviewed him that "some bad things happened, but we won't talk about them." He didn't, and several Lane children have told me that neither of their parents would let them talk about "bad things." So this writer never pressed for those "things," just accepted what some wanted to tell.

Terry Neal heard from his dad one horrific tale of a black man's fate in East Texas, but the main advice Terry had from Duffy Neal was "Don't rock the boat." Duffy had a good business and a good reputation in Crane, and he, like many wise parents in our northwest corner, deliberately worked at making the transition from the bad happenings to the "good life" (relatively, of course) that they had in Crane.

The results of this wisdom and the iron hand of discipline prepared their children to get along very well in our black-and-white world.

THE WALL THAT FAILED

A favorite place to see these people "getting along" is on Facebook, where all races, many individuals who started classes in segregated schools and hardly knew one another then, are now talking about everything from prayer needs to new recipes to birthday parties with a naturalness that pays no mind to most distinctions we older folks grew up with.

Just recently one of my black friends was rejoicing and thanking so many people who had shown love and concern during her recent illness. When she said on Facebook that this is a wonderful, loving place, many respondents agreed with her.

So I can only suspect but will never really know about the bad things that happened to my black friends because they were black, and what worse things must have happened to their forebears.

It was just life, seemed a good one at the time for white southern children whose black caretakers were dearly loved but completely taken for granted. Now they don't know what to make of it and are still pained by it.

The black heritage, under slavery and then segregation/discrimination, was to be very deferential and courteous toward whites. But I don't believe that's the only reason that, when the light at the end of their tunnel began to brighten and then finally began shining on their rights, they were more appreciative of getting those God-given and constitutionally-given rights than they were bitter about having had to wait so long. Appreciation seems inbred.

---

31 Sir Edmund Clark.
32 Larry Copeland, "For Blacks, A Return to Southern Roots." *USA Today*, July 1, 2011.
33 Nancy Griffin, "Morgan Freeman: Home Again," *AARP: The Magazine* 50, no. 6A (November/December 2007): 46–51, 90.

READER'S NOTES

Let no man despise thy youth; but be thou an example ...
—1 Timothy 4:12 KJV

Chapter 8

TALES FOR ENRICHMENT

Our basic story is told.

Certainly not everything. As more than one interviewee has said, to tell the whole story would be too painful. And so we move on.

But for the enrichment of that basic story I must share two more sets of narratives: these first are from local interviewees who frankly want to talk about their integration experiences, to the edification of listeners like me. These additional accounts add depth to their history, and their dialogue—phrasing and vocabulary, starts and stops—add a reality I don't want to keep to myself.

That is why a minimum of editing has been done to their quotes—to let the personalities and emotions shine through their commentary.

Then the next two chapters go beyond Crane County, to convey the universality of this American situation across the whole southern part of our land. First, it's far beyond, into different decades and different states, to show the kinship of grown-up children of white patronage during intensely segregated days.

Then, it's east and west as I tell personal observations of friends who went through the same integration metamorphoses as I and many of my associates did.

Here again I have sense that this "lifetime book" became so because the more I learned, the more I remembered and the more I found out. The learning became more intriguing than the writing, and I was off on another query, another investigation, and another conjecture that led to another interview.

Earliest conversations with local friends on our race history were almost incidental, as we trod lightly out of consideration for each other's feelings. Then as we sensed the mutual desire to communicate honestly, we went higher and deeper in those conversations.

From that first visit from Terry Neal, to a conversation with former journalism students, to reunion talks with other former students, this story was an ever-increasing obsession. I first told it in a paper for the Mosaic of Texas Cultures at Abilene Christian University, and that led to a paper for the Permian Historical Society, and that led to one for the Texas Folklore Society. Always an ultimate goal was this more complete work. And always old friends as well as a few new ones were eager to help, especially my grown-up former students.

One reason I often cite for being so long on this book is that the interviews became so intriguing and personally enlightening. Nearly every time I sat down to write, I decided I needed to pursue a subject further with someone, or thought of another person I wanted to talk with. Each additional interview was liable to change the tone and direction of a chapter or a passage.

Terry Neal—The Starter

Tall and very nice-looking, Terry plays an excellent Buffalo Soldier in a documentary film shown at Fort Davis. I know he felt a deep pride in modeling one of the black troops, as his respect for his forebears is exceeded only by his determination to do what he can to right the wrongs that he can in the here and now.

He has an adamant earnestness in asserting this view, for which he has been accused of having "a chip on his shoulder." He knows this—actually told me about it himself.

Perhaps that is why he left Crane not long after high school, determined never to return, at least to live. But he did, and I'm glad, as he and his lovely wife (actually *named* Lovey) and two daughters became active participants in the community and school for several years.

Terry had come by to ask whether I would support him if he ran for mayor. The answer was yes, and so we began talking, casually for the first time since he was in high school, and seriously for the first ever.

Conversation moved into recollections from our school days and then into some personal revelations that surprised and touched us both. The longer we talked, the more each realized how much he had to learn about the other's past and present feelings and fears, reactions and regrets.

I thought, if Terry and I, who had been in Crane schools before, during and after integration, did not know these things about each other, how many people did? Because the revelations increased our mutual empathy and respect, our story might do the same for others. Other conversations followed.

"Lovey tells me I must forgive everything," he said in one talk.

"Everything" would include many rebuffs because of his color.

Hearing that a stock boy was needed at a local grocery store, he had called the store and was told to come in to apply. He cleaned up, walked to town and the store, and back to the owner's office. But upon looking up from his desk at Terry, the owner said there was a mistake, that he didn't have a job opening. So Terry walked back home.

Other hurts to forgive include events already told, like being turned away from the homecoming dance because of his color.

But standing back a little and down the road in time, one can see those events as strength and courage builders for the service Terry could do, not just for the blacks but for the whole of Crane. Though he knows the younger generation doesn't have much interest, he never tires of talking about his life and times. A wonderful coincidence gave him a forum for just that.

A while back, he and I had an appointment to meet at Crane's museum for discussion. It happened to be a day that Ray Ifera, high school history teacher who always works to make history real, had scheduled his classes to tour the museum. When he discovered Terry, we knew it was a perfect opportunity to give his students some firsthand insights. For these black, white, and brown kids, segregation was mostly in the old annals of history.

So Ifera introduced Terry by telling students when this guy was nineteen years old he was a lifeguard at the black swimming pool. Eyebrows went up—these kids knew only swimming pool, not black or white pools.

"Anybody heard that story about integrating the swimming pools?" Ifera asked. "Maybe not. Terry is an example of how one person can bring about change."

With a gentlemanly grin, Terry began tentatively.

"I didn't expect to do this today. This is kind of a celebrity status for me. I just came over to talk to Mrs. Stroder about her book, you know."

Then he asked whether the students wished to ask questions first. They were giving him undivided attention, hardly knowing what to expect but certainly not knowing enough to ask questions at this point. So he jumped right into trying to convey something his listeners could hardly relate to.

> Growing up in Crane, Texas, at that time was really, really different.
>
> It was the time of Jim Crow laws and segregation. In the courthouse, water fountains were labeled "Colored" and "White." Really you weren't supposed to be in there without someone older if you were black. And not supposed to be across Sixth Street after ten o'clock at night.
>
> The thing that got me involved happened with a black girl named Lawanza Mitchell. She cut herself on a broken toilet at the pool house and she was bleeding. Well, now, in this time, if you were black and you hurt yourself, you just nurse it the best you can. We tried

THE WALL THAT FAILED

to get the blood stopped by applying towels and direct pressure to stop the bleeding, and just sent her home. Back then there wasn't very much for black kids to do because the youth centers were segregated—everything was segregated. If you're black, you stayed over here; if you're white you stayed over there. Hispanic kids, they had it a little bit different because they could go pretty well where they wanted.

Lawanza came back to the pool and asked couldn't we do something about this? I was working for an oil company at the time. I had gone to college one year on a football scholarship and come back to Crane. Man, I thought I had the world by the ear because I had a job with an oil company—though I only got that because of Affirmative Action.[34] I had just married. My wife, Lovey, was from Midland, which was a little different from Crane. In Midland at that time, blacks could go anywhere they wanted, though they were still treated about the same as we were. Anyway, we decided we would try to get the swimming pools and facilities equal for all kids.

I went to a certain commissioner and said, "Why can't we have kids go where they want to go?" And he said, "Well, first you're gonna lose your job because we're not gonna have you watching over those little white girls in swimsuits." I'd had that summer lifeguard job since I was a high school freshman. He was threatening me.

Later the commissioner told a more authentic-sounding, or so he must have thought, reason for segregation.

He told me, "We've never integrated because the nine or ten major oil companies here don't want the blacks and the whites to integrate. They want you blacks down there on this side, and they want the white kids over on this side."

I learned the headquarters for Gulf Oil was in Pennsylvania, so I called up there and asked, "Why do you want the swimming pools segregated in this little town?" I'll never forget his name, Jimmy Lee, an official of Gulf Oil. In 1974 an ordinary person could still pretty well talk to anyone in high places.

He said, "Well, young man, we just send tax money every year to Crane County because we have oil royalties there, but we're not interested in where the money goes." But he did say the company had never made specifications of any kind about segregation.

So I went to the commissioner and told him that. He seemed amazed that this kid had enough about him to find this out. I knew he had earlier said, "Before any of you little nigger [sic] kids go to that white swimming pool (I'm just telling it like it was), I'll hire J. B. Rogers [local construction company] to cement the swimming pool and nobody will ever go swimming again." That's what he said.

But that was just a challenge to me, 'cause I didn't have sense enough to be afraid of him. I thought I was invincible—you find out pretty quick that you're not, especially if you don't get an education, and that's what all you need. [An aside Terry often throws into conversations with young people.]

But this rocked on, and they had meetings all over town, saying blacks are really in an uproar. White people said, "We're all kind of proud of our blacks. They'd never raise anything with anybody. They're quiet. But this nineteen-year-old hell-raiser's got everybody in an uproar."

> That was me. So imagine how I felt—man, I'm a little status symbol around here in Crane, but I'm really nobody, 'cause nobody knew about me. Understand now that very dark blacks like me got segregation from their own people. Also, if your dad didn't work for the school or for the county or at one of the car dealers, then you were like blackballed. So I was segregated by whites because I'm dark and by some blacks 'cause I'm darker.
>
> That summer a guy came down here from—I think Pennsylvania—and told city and county leaders, "We don't care about where this tax money goes, but you do these people an injustice by telling them what you did." I think that was James Lee. He had flown into the Midland/Odessa airport and was here for just a little while and then he left and that was it.

Whoever the official was, it seems the better part of wisdom that he never sought out or communicated personally with Terry. Maybe it was just business, but I rather think he was perceptive enough not to add any more quotable details to the burden of the young man who had called with a question that deserved a definitive response. The official brought that response directly to some people who knew not that they knew not. But now they all knew, and were compelled, not by a nineteen-year-old but by one who represented an economic force in this totally oil-based town—*because* of a nineteen-year-old.

Others who came to Crane on this matter included some NAACP representatives, but Terry saw no real help there.

> They came down here from Midland. This lady was kind of like Jesse Jackson, or maybe Al Sharpton, advocates for black people and supposedly civil rights leaders for everybody. But they seemed to feel, "This is not a big city problem, so let those people work it out themselves." Also, local authorities' idea was still,

"Let's keep our blacks as they are," so the NAACP didn't see any true picture of what was actually going on.

They did, unbeknownst to local blacks, threaten a lawsuit against Crane County and officials, schools, the superintendent of schools, and so on. All kept it hush, hush.

Some blacks didn't think highly of me. They said, "Well, we got everything like we want it here—we work for the county, we've always done good, and now here you come back from school and you're a troublemaker."

But then things got a little better. I grew up in Crane, and it was kind of with me. I couldn't get out, though I tried to a couple of times. I had a football scholarship to Texas Tech, but I left and I came back. Now I guess it was a godsend that I did. Some [white] people in Crane were really good to blacks. But they were kind of like—"I'm gonna treat you good right now, but I'm not gonna let other white people know I'm treating you good, you know."

Now this all happened before you kids were around, and I feel like an old man. I'm fifty-seven years old, and I don't often get to tell my story. Both of my kids graduated from high school here, and Mr. Ifera taught 'em both. Mrs. Stroder taught me. She told me one night, "Terry, what could I do? Charles and I had young kids, and I'm just one person, but I feel bad about it." I said, "I don't know anything you could do, Mrs. Stroder. You didn't create this animal."

But what I have to tell you guys is just be glad of what you are. It doesn't matter whether you're black, green, white, yellow. We're all created equal.

THE WALL THAT FAILED

Here Terry paused for emphasis. Ifera continued the swimming pool story.

> In the summer of '69 I worked as a lifeguard at the swimming pool, segregated then. But the next year when the season was about to start, at a city council meeting, one commissioner—I remember his words pretty clearly—said, "Well, Terry is not gonna back off, so we'll have to integrate." They decided to close what had been the black pool.
>
> By then Terry had the law on his side. That Civil Rights Act of 1964 made what they were doing illegal. A lot of southern towns hung on for a long time, violating the law. It just took a lawsuit threat to get some to make the change.

Terry said he really didn't know he had that much clout.

"In those days," he said, "if you raised as much hell—I'm just telling you like it was—as I did, you might wind up dead somewhere. But after we got the publicity going, I think they were afraid then to do anything because I might not be the only person they had to take on."

Ifera mentioned that Terry's dad had a garage and said that Terry might not have as much at stake personally because he was young and could leave town if he wanted to, but Duffy Neal's business depended on the goodwill of the people in town.

"Yes, my dad's a mechanic," Terry said, "a good mechanic. He was called Nigger Duffy. He worked on people's cars and just rolled with the punches. He was glad to be here, and he did what he wanted to do pretty well and had a good life in Crane."

Ray moved the focus a little.

"Terry and his wife," he said, "were the first black family to have a house outside of the black part of town."

Terry told about that.

Yeah, we moved across town. Now during that time, if you were black, after a certain time of the evening you needed to be on that [northwest] side of Sixth Street and behind that wall down there. I don't know if you guys know where that wall is? But Lovey and I, when we moved here, we lived on Eleventh Street, in a house owned by the only man that would rent to us.

It was Arnold Durham, and he later told me he had got ridiculed for renting to me. Some people wanted to just run him out of town on a rail because people labeled me as a troublemaker, and someone said, "You rent to that boy (that's what usually they called us back then, boys) and it's just gonna make things worse."

But we stayed. Not only that, but we moved around the corner to another place, and it was worse then. It seemed the more you got up there around Lena Drive, the worse it was. So we just stayed there for a while. I left Crane again I think in '04 for work, and my wife stayed here until she retired with the school system, where she worked in the cafeteria.

Terry said he often reflected on those times.

Asked to tell a little about his mother, he smiled and nodded. Then he repeated the tale I'd heard from Billy Joe, that some teachers thought they were doing Clara Neal, who babysat their children, a favor by not demanding enough of the Neal children.

But that was not satisfactory. Terry's mom insisted he repeat the first grade and learn what he was supposed to.

"And I did," he said, "and I guess it really helped me, but my mother did not play. A teacher told me once, 'If you don't straighten up, young man, I'm gonna bring your mother up here.' I said, 'You don't want my mother to come up here. If she does, I'm gonna get whipped for not doing what I'm supposed to do and you're probably gonna get chastised for not doing what you're supposed to do.'"

THE WALL THAT FAILED

Ray asked that Terry explain what he had learned about the origin of his dark skin.

Okay. During the slavery days if you were a fair-skinned black, then you got to work up to the house with the white people because they thought that all dark-skinned black people were really evil. The darker-skinned black people were more directly from Africa and the light-skinned were [often] mulattos. [a mulatto is a person born from one black parent and one white parent, or a person of mixed white and black ancestry in any proportion.]

Now you kids ever heard of a concubine? In those days the white slave owners, the white women, were only for having kids and carrying their name on. Now when the slave owner had sexual desires, he went and got him a concubine, one of the black women, to sleep with him. So that's how a lot of light-skinned blacks came about.

I didn't know until about six months ago that we are Mandingoes. My cousin is doing a family tree, and he said, "You came from the Mandingo tribe in Africa." They called big black men bucks, and our family came from bucks that bred other slaves.

We were in San Francisco, California, and I was getting ready for my aunt's funeral and it was kind of strange. I was at the kitchen sink, and my cousin said, "Answer the door." I said, "Looks like some white people."

So she came to the window and looked out and said, "Let those people in, son. Those are your first cousins." Man, they looked like you, Mr. Ifera, blew me away. Now here I am, I had to get to be nearly sixty years old, and I'm finding I got a white boy that looks like me and my family that I can call Cuz. But that came from the slave owners. You know, was it Thomas Jefferson we found out later on had all these black people in his family? That's where that came from.

"Isn't there still that discrimination today," Ray asked, "among black people about skin tone?"

Terry agreed but used the opportunity to admonish the younger generation.

> Kids now, they're getting away from it. But black kids don't even know their history. They don't even want to know. They're too busy being in gangs and smoking all the weed they can, you know. I feel sorry for our black kids that don't even know who they are. And they look at me like an old man that—uh, nobody I know.
>
> Donny Bishop—any of you guys know Donny? Yes, he's a big football celebrity here. And he used to say, "Uncle Terry, it couldn't have been that bad." Uh, yeah, it was that bad. It was worse. When your own people [look down on you because you are dark]—man, you're kind of like a man without a country. And that may have been what drove me to try to find out who I was. You start digging in your history, you'll be surprised to find who you really are.

"Look at Michael Jackson," Ifera said. "He kept getting lighter and lighter and—" Terry gave his take on that.

> He did that through surgery. You know he had a flared nose and dark skin. The whiter you could be or look, the better off you were in society. I think that's why he did it, 'cause I read some on him. Especially

> when he got to be a celebrity and he could be whoever he wanted to be. He could be outside of Michael.
>
> His dad had beat him, and he had a really sad childhood. I don't know if that kid ever got to be a kid. But later he ruined himself lightening his skin and making himself or trying to be white. A lot of black people did that then. A lot of black people passed [a term meaning pass for white]. I knew some people that did that. During the day they would pass for white but at night they would be in the black section of town. They were light enough to pass either way, you know. I never was. You can look at me and tell what I am right away.

Ifera said it's interesting to compare different generations' views.

"Your father saw what happened to the black man, and that made an impression on him, but you couldn't see it quite the same way, and it's even less with the next generation of blacks. And if they don't know the history, then they don't understand why—"

Terry cut in.

> They don't know and they don't care, but then it's good that they don't, a lot of 'em. They grow up feeling that they're equal, so they are. Because kids now, they don't care whether I'm green, you know. They're not gonna listen to me anyway. It's just kind of like, "This old man, he's sitting here telling us all this stuff, you know."
>
> But [some white] kids back then were taught that black people are evil, they're mean—don't be around them.

The students still were silent but very attentive, so Terry and Ifera and I chatted for their benefit about racial incidents through the years.

We spoke of Diane Wright, first black student to be elected president of the student council, in 1975, and her brother who became a medical doctor.

Ifera told about their father, Bethune principal with probably the highest education of anybody in the school system, who at the time of integration was assigned an aide's job at the elementary school.

Terry told of a prejudicial reaction in the spring Coronation of Favorites, how there was uproar from some parents that some black boys were escorting white girls and the like. The students, only embarrassed about the matter, worked out an arrangement on their own to placate the older generation.

Next Terry told of a teacher who he thought encouraged and helped some students burn a cross in the northwest neighborhood when certain blacks received special honors.

> Can you imagine that? Waking up about three o'clock in the morning and seeing a cross made out of tow sacks, in your neighborhood about thirty foot in the air and burning. And then there were all those little rocks with notes on 'em about what's gonna happen if blacks do this and blacks do that. And then you go to school and you're looking around like, "I wonder who did that." And you think about their parents. It's sad to say, but a lot of those old people had to die out for things to get better in Crane.

"Well, I told some of these stories in history class," Ifera said, "but I'm glad you were here because it makes it real when students can see and hear the person these things really happened to."

Then Ifera told students about the fifteen-minute movie in the Visitors' Center at Fort Davis.[35]

"If you'll look at that movie the next time you're down there, you'll see Terry Neal in a Buffalo Soldier's uniform. He starred as an extra."

"And no," Terry said, "I haven't made any money yet. That's how smart I am."

Asked to relate a positive experience in closing, Terry told of a Safety Patrol trip when he was in middle school. The annual trip was underwritten by the Volunteer Fire Department, and VFD members as well as school teachers accompanied the students.

> We [members of the Safety Patrol] went to Hemisfair in San Antonio. Mr. Stroder kind of took me under his wings, and you knew right away that Mr. Stroder didn't feel like some whites did. But he had to let some other people think that he did, that he did not care for [us].
>
> That whole weekend he and Bill Estes [middle school principal] and one other man [Arlen Carroll, Crane postmaster] took care of me. The whole weekend they made sure I felt welcome and wasn't just ostracized like, like we were in Crane. I'll never forget that. Whenever people do things for you, you'd better tell someone, because it molds you as a person and shows, you know, who cares about you.
>
> And you have another such man right here, Mr. Ifera.

Terry described Mr. Ifera's fair-mindedness and classroom thoughtfulness.

"I have people all the time walk up to me and ask about some of my experiences that Mr. Ifera told them.

"That's probably all I have today," Terry said. "Sometimes you get tired of talking about yourself. When I told my daughter this morning that I was coming down here to talk to Mrs. Stroder, she said, 'Aren't you about tired of beating that horse, Dad?'"

"But that's how you keep history alive," Ifera said.

As the class prepared to leave, Terry added a postscript.

One thing I do admire of these kids today is they see each other for who they are. They don't care that this young lady over here is black or you got a green shirt on, you know what I'm saying? Am I right? You don't care. In my time they couldn't be like that because their parents wouldn't let 'em: you don't associate with blacks because they're substandard to you and—but kids now are so curious, like my grandson. He doesn't care what color anybody is, and that's the way I want him to be.

"That's a good note to end this on," Ifera said.

Annette Lane and Louie Jones—Still Journalism Buddies

I often group these two together for characterization. Their friendship has been consistent since high school. They gave me my first recorded session for these stories, told in chapter 4, and I have relied on them jointly for so many perspectives, as well as tasks.

Louie majored in journalism at Angelo State University, intending to be a journalism teacher, but later earned his master's degree at Texas Tech and administered service programs in several areas. Severe health problems caused him to come home to Crane in the nineties.

Annette has remained in Crane. Both Louie and Annette have worked off and on for the local weekly newspaper and have collaborated on some stories of local history.

Our first conversation became a program for the Permian Historical Society and then an article in the PHS Annual. Beyond the accounts of their middle school integration memories, they reflected on other views of race relations.

Annette said that she never knew there was a wall until we were ready to dedicate the marker. She said a group discussed this at the last school reunion.

THE WALL THAT FAILED

> After I left the ceremony and went to Jerry Smith's party. L. V. Tennison, Mike Warren, Linda Thackeray and Jerry—a whole bunch of us—were sitting around discussing this. L. V. said he didn't remember a wall either. So many of us didn't. I guess I thought that had been a wall around a house or a business. I said, "I don't remember Crane being prejudiced. Why are people saying that it was, in the paper?" You know, in the Odessa paper they wrote it up so ugly, about the wall. I remember thinking, *That's not Crane—not the Crane I remember.*
>
> L. V. said the only [racial] thing he remembered from high school was the homecoming hassle about mixed couples. I was in choir with some of the girls, and I know the problem was seen only by the parents. So that's the only thing we remembered that was negative.

Louie referred to the valedictorian incident, and he and Annette agreed that it was mostly political and certainly beyond students' control.

"How unfortunate it was," Annette said, "that Billy Van had to graduate that first year. I'm sure that by the next year things might have been different."

"They might have." Louie tried to be philosophical with his friend. Annette spoke of her position with her children.

> I've always told my kids that they are red, white, and blue. You are not black, you're not Spanish, and you're not white. You're red, white, and blue. And I have never had any problems with my kids. Never.
>
> I have a daughter, half-black—well, both my children are half-black, but one looks like A. J., and one looks like me. We got one of each.

> They never came to me and said, "Mom, why did—?" My children never had any problems in Crane High School—not with the teachers, not with the students. I don't know whether it was because they lived in a more accepting world.
>
> Some draw attention to what they are—"I'm black, so I deserve this." Or, "I'm Hispanic, and I deserve this." To me, you work for it. And that's what I always told the kids. It's not what you are; it's who you are. I was lucky in that with my children. They never cried to me and said, "Why did you make me?" I know a girl who had a son who hated her when he grew up because he was half-black. I don't know if it was the way she raised him. I didn't know her very well, and I don't know how their life went, but he hated her—stopped speaking to her.

I told them that I believe most teachers, on the whole, felt bad about segregation but didn't know what to do about it. So when Rosa Parks and others paved the way, here we were in the wings waiting to make integration work.

Annette said that's the way she felt.

> If my daddy had [lived] in this time, he would have been an activist. But back then, he was just a poor laborer. He wasn't even my father, but my stepfather, but he married my mother and adopted me when I was nine months old.
>
> Never went to school a day in his life, and that man could read and write, work a flower bed, paint, or build anything. He taught himself everything. As he was growing up, different people took him in, and he was thankful for them all. He always taught me—"When someone reaches out to you, don't care what color their skin is. And when you reach out to

somebody, don't look to see what color the hand is that's reaching back to you is. Take it." He was a very wise man. But nowadays, the kids—they don't have a clue.

"They take so much for granted," Louie said, "because of the time they grew up. You and I were at that big transition period—big transition. We came together in a kind of melting pot."

Annette said that period was the culmination of the Civil War to her.

"Lincoln set the slaves free, but almost nobody until the sixties started mingling freely."

The day before this recording, there had been a walkout of Spanish people across Texas, in protest of new or proposed immigrations laws. Annette talked with a grin about her son.

> Cris, my youngest, had to work yesterday, and he kept calling me and saying, "Do you think I should strike? Do you think I should walk out?" He was just joking with me because he knew I'd think that was ridiculous.
>
> He said, "I think I'm going to the movies. What do you think?"
>
> I said, "I think you'd better get to work."
>
> "Oh, okay."
>
> It was so funny, because he thinks it just hilarious, what some people did yesterday. They think they're protesting for the Spanish people, and they've got it all wrong.

Louie said it reminded him, though, of the protests and demonstrations and marches in the sixties.

"But we were legal," she said. "That's the difference."

Louie agreed.

Annette remembered protesting the Vietnam War.

> I don't remember anything I didn't protest. And Jill Rodgers. We were just protesters. It was just that time, that peace-loving time. You didn't want war. Rita Seabourn's brother was in Viet Nam, and we were in gym when it came over the news that the war was over. We went crazy—we were just kids, didn't know what was wrong, didn't have a clue what was going on in Nam. We just believed it was wrong.

Soon talk returned to the subject of prejudice. Louie said the prejudice he saw in Crane was in the failure to hire black teachers.

> I know a number of students who graduated here and then from college, who have applied for jobs and didn't get any response whatever. I graduated from Crane High School in 1971, and I graduated from Angelo State in 1976, around Christmas time. I remember putting in an application. I never heard anything. It was as if it didn't happen. I never got a call saying, "We want to interview you," or, "We don't want to interview you"—not a word.
>
> It's just natural that you apply at your home school first. That's all you know. It is a good school, and I think I learned a lot from being here, but there is a problem.
>
> I don't know if they think we're incompetent, or—but I think we're just as competent as some other teachers that we've had.

I mentioned that Janet (Lane) Collins had recently been hired, and I recalled Superintendent Joe Allen's saying that any daughter of Jack Lane's is bound to be high quality.

Annette said that many companies don't hire full-time.

"I don't know if it saves benefits, or what, but they just want to hire people by contract."

THE WALL THAT FAILED

True to the manner of these two to disagree agreeably, Louie said he didn't think that had anything to do with hiring black teachers in Crane, Texas.

"They're not hiring white teachers on contract," he said. "They hire white teachers every year."

Then he told that he had never wanted to teach after his practice teaching experience.

> I did my student teaching in San Angelo under Ed Cole. I was so looking forward to working under him. I taught journalism and yearbook, half a day.
>
> I remembered Mr. Cole from our high school journalism gatherings. He remembered me and some of the mischievous things I had done in summer workshops and contests and conventions.
>
> But while I was doing my student teaching, Mr. Cole got sick and died. There was nobody to replace him. In essence, I replaced him, because they didn't have a full-time teacher.
>
> So I was burned out before I started.
>
> It was horrible—it was a big responsibility. I was in college, and this was a huge school, and I had the responsibility of the newspaper and the yearbook. They hired a new teacher, a kind of a substitute who knew less than I, and they wanted me to be there all day, because there was no one else. And I got burned out. A few of those kids were dedicated, really wanted to do a good job—but the journalism department had their own building, off to ourselves. Most kids wanted to smoke cigarettes out around the building. They didn't even want to come into class.
>
> I said if I got through this, I would never teach again.[36]

But soon as he attended graduate school at Texas Tech, he helped with Project Upward Bound, a summer program to help minority children transition from high school to college.

"I really fell in love with those kids," he said. "They were all special to me. Most were college-bound kids, grasping for—What do I do? How do I do it? That was refreshing to me, after the fiasco I had at Central. That was a real rewarding job."

We talked about the wall and its implications, Annette saying she and her parents often went to the Dew-Drop Inn in the northwest section but never noticed the wall.

Louie spoke of tearing down the wall, and then talk moved to the marker dedications. Louie said he originally thought it was ridiculous to memorialize that wall.

"In my mind," he said, "you don't try to build up bad things. It represented a bad time. It never had any effect on me, but I knew what it stood for, and it was not the kind of thing that I would want to memorialize. But I went along with the group."

Annette thought it was a way to say this generation doesn't feel this way, so we want to acknowledge that it happened.

Louie told of how a group of black folks met the night before the marker dedications, some wanting to boycott the program. Then Louie asked whether anyone had seen the plaques, and they had not, so went to look.

"Everything changed," he said. "It was softer than we had thought. It was almost an apology Even though we had agreed earlier that it should be done, we feared it hadn't been done right. But after we read the plaque at Bethune, attitudes changed. We felt very good."

"It's hard," Annette observed, "to apologize for someone else. We're not prejudiced, but it is hard to atone for someone else; you don't know the words to do it with. It's not like something we had done—I'm sorry about this and I take it back."

THE WALL THAT FAILED

Jo Ann: Need a Little Color

"We need some diversity on the council—got to add some color there."

That slogan helped Jo Ann Davenport win a seat on the student council when she was a freshman, and it seems to have become part of her personal and political creed ever since.

Everywhere she goes, she said people know she is from Crane, Texas, and that's where she learned the value, according to her own words, of people of all colors working together for everyone's good.

Perhaps her take-charge personality, her leadership, got its start that freshman year. A family emergency about the same time helped.

> My dad was in Albuquerque for a kidney transplant, and my mom was with him, so I had to step up and play mother to four brothers and sisters. We were literally by ourselves. My great-grandmother was across the street, and my grandmother down the street. So I had family all around, but in the house we were by ourselves.
>
> During that period—I had always been friends with guys, even in my class. Guys were my best friends. They were nothing more, you know. I mean all of 'em had girlfriends, but to them I was just another one of the fellas. And you know after volleyball practice I'd have to cook supper for my four brothers and sisters. Guys like Willie and Ronald, they would come to the house, and they would be sitting at the kitchen table, and we'd just be cutting up just having a good time.
>
> Well, to the older generation that was very disrespectful—"She's just a fast little girl and she has no manners and bla, bla, bla—" but my grandmother would come over, and nothing was happening. I mean I was cooking supper, and I would say, "You all

want to eat?" and I let my friends eat, and they'd go home. The deal was—rule of thumb, at ten o'clock everybody else's out and we're there by ourselves But to the people in the outside looking in, you know, "She's young and she has all those young boys over their house and—."

My mama would call every night, and I would give her the day's activities. Being intimate with those boys was the farthest thing from my mind. My brothers and sisters that I've got to make sure go to school, get fed—that was my top priority.

I'll never forget when my mom did come back and different little ladies would say, "I just can't believe it, these guys were over at your house."

My mom would say, "Well, I trust my children." And they were like, "How could you, how could you let her have all those guys over to the house?" Well, my mom said, "Because I know that she has good home training and she knows what's right and wrong and there's some things she just wouldn't do."

There was this one lady that said she didn't want her daughter being friends with me because I just wasn't a nice girl, and this other lady didn't want her son around me. It really hurt my feelings because they were looking at me like that and they didn't even know me. When you grow up in a community like Crane, it's so small and everybody knows everything, but these ladies ....

And when my mom came home, naturally I shared everything with her, and she was like, "Don't worry about it." My dad was a deacon in the church, and he would say, "I'm not worried about it 'cause I know my kids."

Then my senior year my mom said I could have a graduation party. So it's the night before graduation.

THE WALL THAT FAILED

> My grandparents owned the Dew-Drop Inn Café. At the front were all those older black people sitting around drinking coffee and eating stuff, and in the back there I'm getting ready for my graduation party.
>
> Fine, so my friends start coming—all these white boys—and the older folks were just—what are they doing here? And here come all these little white girls. Well, the white girls, they were so nervous—"If my mother only knew I was here in this café, I'd probably get in trouble." They were so uneasy they left early, but oh, we had a ball. They danced, they danced, they stayed forever, and all these elderly black people—like Ernest Hollins and my great-grandmother—just couldn't believe I did that.
>
> My grandmother told me to come there a minute. "Why did you—?" "What—all these are my friends." I'll never forget my granddad. He said, "Oh, Lord I know there's gonna be a fight, Grandma. We're gonna be in trouble. If a certain commissioner could see this—oh my God."
>
> Then after everybody left and we were cleaning up, someone with my grandmother said, "You just don't do that. That's a no-no. They have their side, and we have our side."

Later some of those ladies commented that Jo Ann would "never amount to nothing," but still her mother said she was not worried about what people say.

"So I was determined," she said. "I'm gonna succeed in life."

So she told that's why, when she moved to Odessa, she started working for the City of Odessa.

> I was working for the City, and I'd see how people were being misused. People would come in to pay their water bill and they just—they weren't treated

fairly. I had flashbacks of when I ran for student council, and thought the Odessa City Council needed some color.

So I talked it in the community, and people said, "Jo Ann, you do a lot of volunteer work and everybody knows you. You work hard in your church, you're in a lot of organizations, so you've kind of paid your dues, so you need to run."

I ran for public office and won, and I'd come back home, and these same old little ladies that had said I wouldn't be nothing, and I was just trampy, I would see them, and at first they wouldn't even halfway look at me.

That really bothered me. Those are the same people that said I would amount to nothing. They were just waiting because they knew I was gonna get pregnant. No, that's not on my agenda. I have a career I want to pursue. I stayed the course and was determined to be successful, and as a result those ladies just kind of treated me different.

Sometimes it was, "Oh, Jo Ann thinks she's it and she thinks she's that." I said, "Wait, what's wrong with this picture? You know, I'm the same person. I'm the same person that these people said was this little nobody, the girl with no manners, no character, reputation gone to shot, and now I think I'm Miss Goody Two Shoes?"

So then politics would start. You know, city council people are always on the news, in the newspaper, and there's one particular lady—I was home and ran into her at the Dollar Store, and she said, "I'm so proud of you 'cause I never really thought you would amount to anything, because some of the things that you did." I said, "What did I do, what did I do? If I had it to do all over again, I would do it because those

THE WALL THAT FAILED

people were my friends. There was nothing out of the ordinary or nothing wrong going on."

I said, "But you know, you didn't even know me, but you judged me, and you know, your kids have done worse than my mother's kids." "Well, you know my kids didn't have the breaks." I said, "That's no excuse. You can be whatever you want in life. It's up to you." So that really hurt me, and even today some of those people are still alive, and when they pass me, you know, it's, "Hi, hi, how you doing?" and they don't have too much conversation for me.

I asked Jo Ann whether she had any negative experiences with integration. Again she spoke plainly and left no doubt of her sincerity.

You know, as I look back—I learned from everyone's experience in my high school years. Whether you like the person or not, the advantage of growing up in a small town of 3,000-plus people, a small community where people were people, was that you had to approach 'em and you had to love 'em for who they were because you couldn't, I mean you couldn't get around [anyone]. They were right there.

There's some that you like more than others, but you had to deal with them all. In high school I didn't have a teacher that I didn't like. Now the principal I'll never forget, Mr. Anderegg. He was so stern. He never smiled, and I always thought, you know, he just don't like black people, he don't like black people, and I don't like him. Well, the more I got to be around him and I got to know him, that was just Mr. Anderegg—that was his style. He was very standoffish and he ruled, you know, with an iron, with a whip—you know, it was this way or no way.

Jo Ann won't be surprised for me to say here that she had something of a reputation for belligerence in high school, just skirting the law, so to speak, with her frankness. But—mainly, I believe, due to parental support that put school authority in the right perspective—she was controllable, in the Crane way.

Stories of her semiconflicts with her volleyball coach and government teacher, told in earlier chapters, prove that professional teachers and strong parents want the same thing for their students, and together can often accomplish it. Now she spoke of both incidents from an adult perspective.

"I was treated the same way at school as at home." And Mr. Stovall's government class fired her interest in politics.

All worth it, she now believes.

Jo Ann is one among many whose memories bring perceived problems of youth into focus as just the growing-up process. Sometimes they can laugh about a recollection more pleasurable than the living was.

Teacher's Memories

Humor in many areas seemed to lighten the atmosphere in early days of integration. Evidence is seen in the fact that counselor Ima Roycroft could tell this story years after the fact, at a reunion of the class of '76. Ronald was in attendance and just grinned as she started speaking.

> So, all you all are really my kids and I've got to tell this on Ronald. When you were talking about, uh, racism a while ago, I couldn't help thinking of it. I had just gotten to Crane and Mr. [Clint] Carroll [former counselor] had died and he hadn't finished up all the schedules. I was recording grades for him when Willie Neal and Ronald Jeffery [both black] came in.

I didn't know Willie and Ronald. I didn't know anybody. And they told me what they wanted and Willie was the one that had the schedule problem. So we took care of that, and when they got ready to leave, I said, "You boys come back and see me." Well, I walk out and Ronald turns on me: he says, "I'm not a boy."

I thought, *Oh, what have I done now?*

And I looked at him and said the first thing that came to mind: "Well, I calls 'em as I sees 'em, Ronald, and you don't look like a girl, so I called you a boy." I thought old Willie would fall out on the floor laughing. Ronald just turned around and walked off. And you know that? That was the last I heard of that from him. He was just Ronald from then on. But man, did I make sure I didn't say "boy" unintentionally. I hadn't meant anything, and I don't know if you were just trying to see what I would do or what, but I was certainly caught off guard.

Lanes and Friends—Diverse in Unity

At a recent all-school reunion, Artha "Cookie" Lane and I found a spot in the student union room for a taping session and reminiscing with Nikki Sheppard, who is white, and Annette Lopez Lane, half-Hispanic and half-white.

These racial distinctions, something matter-of-fact but matter-of-no-concern to the participants, are inserted here to help give the flavor of our relationships and our conversations for the reader. These were old friends, gathered at the request of an old teacher to help with data for her book and for the oral history library records, and yet it was spontaneous reunion conversation.

Race relations was discussed as part of our history, part of our past, something to be remarked on and viewed with wonder at some times, yet in a spirit of camaraderie.

"Remember when—" someone would say, and they would be off and running with another experience.

Annette referred to the closeness of the black community in general and the Lane family in particular, and Cookie carried the ball. Fifty-seven Lanes had attended the last family reunion. That would include some Joneses, as Johnnie May Jones is Jack Lane's sister, and many others. Reunions take place every five years, at a location chosen by the organizer of that year's event.

Patriarch Jack Lane never misses the gathering, Cookie said, but his love for his home sometimes throws a hitch in things. At a certain time, before anyone else makes the move to return home, he has his bag packed and is clearly waiting for his ride.

"There is no changing him," Cookie said, "and though he waits patiently, someone feels compelled to get him back to Crane."

Cookie told a special thing about her father's reaction to his daughters' weddings.

"Always on the day of the wedding, he was going about some routine, like watering the backyard or the like, until someone came out and said, 'Daddy, it's time to get ready and go to the church.'

"Then at the church and even as we started down the aisle, he was saying, 'Remember, baby, you can always come home. You can always come home.'"

We challenged Cookie to name all her siblings, in order. Quickly Annette and Nikki chimed in here and there when they thought one was out of order, but she did it. They are Bobby, Ellis, Cookie, Kathy, Johnny, Sunny, Kay, Daisy, Georgia, Joyce, Vickie, Jeannette, Carolyn, Robby, Blondie. One daughter died in infancy. The other fourteen are all living,

Louie came in to take a picture during this conversation, and then we wound up by saying that there should be a Bethune reunion at the next all-school reunion.

THE WALL THAT FAILED

Cookie does a little substitute teaching these days, and is "a part of everything," though she attended and graduated from the Bethune School before integration. So by consensus it was agreed that she would be the one to promote such a minireunion, like the various class-by-year reunions, at the next all-school gathering.

Old Cranes have always come to reunions, and with today's electronic communications, it is easier to get the word around, and the flocks fly in.

Just as stories flew in when we asked on P&G Nuggets for input on the wall and integration.

You can take the girl out of Crane, but you can't take Crane out of the girl—or the boy. Anyone who thinks so might put out an appeal for Crane stories, any subject, to find old Craneites coming out of the woodwork with stories. On e-mail, blog, even snail mail or by telephone.

It's understandable that very few black ex-students participated in responses on the e-mail Crane news line, *Purple and Gold Nuggets*. It was begun by Jeff Henderson, fifties grad, as essentially a reminiscence and update place for his contemporaries in our segregated school. It steadily expanded, but so far not many blacks have picked up on it.

Elsewhere, though, Cookie Lane and other blacks have largely shown the same nostalgic love for their upbringing, beginning in the very strict Bethune community, the northwest corner, as that expressed by white students we hear from. What a place to grow up.

Time for another disclaimer: In no way does this work claim there were not glitches, glaring imperfections, and glossed-over wrongs in this town as in others, especially with regard to our main focus—segregation/integration and the aftermath. But a close look at some of the characters shows we have much to build on.

So we acknowledge the negatives while focusing on the positives. Terry said he had never wanted to live in Crane so long but is glad he did. Cookie never attended Crane High School but calls it her school too, now. Her adjust-and-be-thankful attitude seen in all the Lanes and others of her generation no doubt came from their parents, who counted better-off as well-enough-off and held tight to a home they had been drawn to by circumstances.

Same with the white folks, with a notable exception. Like many blacks, they had never thought much about the wall and segregation, just knew that was the way it was. But most white children from those days I have talked with first express wonder that they seldom wondered about segregation, then they question why, and then they are eager to tell tales of a few good relations with blacks over the years. Today some are working in their own ways to accept, acknowledge, and appreciate all interracial relationships.

Online

When the wall subject started appearing on *P&G Nuggets*, input poured into *Nuggets,* mostly from and about those grown-up white kids of segregation days. Their comments open windows on attitudes of both races, over two or three generations.

A recurring theme in these comments is white teenagers who accepted other races and adults who didn't.

Bill Marlowe, who would graduate in 1949, moved to town as a child and experienced "qualified" black-white relations. He recently wrote some of his experiences.

> My father set up and ran a Pontiac/Cadillac dealership in conjunction with an oil field welding shop in Crane. He hired a Negro mechanic, Duffy Neal, and that exposed him to criticism and hate which I witnessed firsthand from some locals. Although Duffy was an excellent mechanic, some people would not let him work on their cars and some even refused to come into the garage where he worked.
>
> During the summer between my sophomore and junior years, I worked for W. D. Porch Construction laying concrete sidewalks, curbs, driveways, and

> home foundations. I was the only white boy on a crew of 14 blacks. I had, and still have, the highest respect for those blacks. But I got all sorts of slurs [from adults] over my summer job—and that made me pretty angry.
>
> Most of my classmates thought nothing of me working with Negros, but it was a different story to be *friends* with them. We have made great strides in getting past the race thing. Wars seldom resolve all political issues. Unfortunately, it takes the dying off of several generations to cleanse hate air.

So true, but I'm happy to observe that some folks of those days—like Bill's dad—did what they could when they could.

Similar philosophical reflections pervade a memory from Teddye Coleman Stephan about her first time in Crane's "colored town," at a worship service.

> For a sheltered child, as most of us were in the days before TV, the memory of bright lights and a deep, loud voice and responses from the crowd remains quite vivid. Dozens of cars had pulled up to a rough stage and scores of people were sitting on the hoods, white faces and black faces listening to a singular message about the Savior. We were there because we'd been invited to hear a Gospel preacher, a man who happened to be black and who happened to be preaching in an outside setting in north Crane. If people had followed the message preached that night, there [might never] have been a wall. If we remember that message, maybe there never will be again.

A New Old Friend from Yankee Land Observes

The readiness of blacks to get on with their lives was recognized with some surprise by my Texan-turned-Yankee friend Margaret Collins. The daughter of a Presbyterian preacher, she grew up and attended school in several different Texas towns, including Crane, where she spent two elementary school years.

Now retired from social work/education career, she lives in Amherst, Massachusetts. Once, at dinner with friends, she heard discussion of *Friday Light Nights,* and about a wall between the races in an oil field town where she had lived.

She remembered little—and nothing of a wall—about Crane, but within the little, two memories stood out. One was the "million-dollar school" her father showed her their first day in town, saying this was why he had chosen to come to this place. The other was that her education in Mrs. Green's fifth-grade class "may very well have been worth a million bucks."

"It still stands apart," Collins wrote, "from some very lousy learning experiences in other little towns as the time I learned the rudiments of grammar."

She had long considered revisiting and writing about towns she had lived in as a child, and when she heard of *FNL,* that thought took shape posthaste. She came to see for herself, found there really was a wall, and also found me—and there began an instant and, I believe, mutually rewarding friendship. In delving into the history of walls and dividing lines and segregation, she has found and shared many resources to my own edification over the last several years.

She had found the wall and said it was nothing like the Berlin type image she had conjured up. But here she was and ready to look into this matter. I gave her some basic material and a number of names, and back home in Amherst she researched and considered and made some telephone calls, wrote some letters. Later she wrote me.

I attempted interviews with African Americans who grew up in Crane and who live in or near it today. There was often reluctance on their part to contribute further information. However, those with whom I spoke are very clear about one thing. The wall did not accomplish its mission. If anything, it taught some very valuable lessons about human nature that have stood over time. I recently spoke with Louie Jones, born in 1953, and in the sixth grade when the schools integrated. He told me he has learned to trust his instincts about people.

"The wall and segregation helped me to realize that everybody isn't the way they should be," he said. "You have to learn to deal with everyone. You learned who your friends were and I had lots of them and [in the end] race didn't matter. The people who built the wall had a choice and for whatever reason they did it, it was there. The people of Crane supported the wall and the developer benefitted."

We discussed the fact that the full story of the wall has never been told. His sentiment about this was plain.

"To tell the full story will cause pain for my people."

Jo Ann Davenport Littleton, head of the Black Council of Odessa, is the daughter of the first African American baby born in Crane. Her stories about the Dew-Drop Inn—a café west of the wall owned by her grandparents Ed and Beulah Mayes—are another enlightening chapter in Crane's history, too lengthy to be written here. Despite criticism from African American relatives who were frightened for her reputation and safety, she had many white friends and became the first black member of the high school student council. She has great fondness for her days in the integrated schools and for many of her white teachers there. The wall did not matter to her.

As I contemplated what Jones and Davenport Littleton were saying, I began to wonder whether this was even a story a white person could or should tell. Certainly not in the manner I originally wished. I looked for every story I could find pointing out how horrible it was as a black to live with this structure. But everywhere I looked, Crane African Americans told me that they were not its victims. And they have moved on.

She looked up and contacted a fifth grade best friend and an old marble-playing buddy to find interesting memories.

Brenda said she had lived in Crane all her life until she went off to college but remembered nil about the wall. Gary's response was a little different He remembered the wall existed but never recalled its being discussed as a 'segregation wall.'

"It just existed," he said. "I played Pony League baseball across the street with black players, including L.V. Miles. At the time, black families attended those games but sat in separate bleachers on the first base line. Black kids did not attend school with us or participate in any [of our] organized [school] sports."

Margaret inferred, from these comments and those of others she had talked with, that white males usually knew more about the wall than females.

"I attribute that to the fact that black and white boys played baseball together. Their parents were forced to sit separately, but they got to know each other, at least during the time they were in the Pony League and Little League games. According to school records, they also scrimmaged in basketball. Girls, for whom Title IX sports equality did not exist, did not have this opportunity."

Margaret's discoveries were noted in *P&G Nuggets* by Judy Googins, my old friend and former student, whose tale of her father's integrated Little League teams is told earlier.

Judy said she had discovered the wall in reading Collins's article and told of a different side she had seen during her ten years in Crane.

> By the time we were in high school, I think most of my generation were oblivious to the [wall's purported meaning]—but perhaps I speak only for the white kids. Nevertheless, it never entered into our conversations, and both Afro-American and Hispanic kids became our friends.

In Novels

Natural acceptance of people and the way things were was the theme of Crane's most prolific writer, Elmer Kelton. After his first schooling by his mother on the ranch, Kelton attended and graduated from Crane schools, taking journalism under—and becoming profoundly influenced by—Paul Patterson.

Encouraged by Patterson, Kelton began writing pulp fiction while still in college at the University of Texas. Then his "day job" as editor of the *West Texas Livestock Weekly* continued many years, and the ranchers he met and interviewed and worked with complemented his ranch upbringing to give his fiction reality of action and believability.

So no wonder he developed characters like Gabe, an African American veteran of the Civil War, riding with white cowboys through a West Texas sundown town that allowed him no quarter.[37]

Similar themes are present in many other works, with characters doing their best to survive during intensely racist times.

In a somewhat different time and a quite different setting, *The Wolf and the Buffalo*[38] chronicles the rise of the black race and decline of the red. Two almost winsome characters, an Indian and a black, come alive to the reader as they live out their types in history, equally strong and perceptive of the way the times are taking them. *Wolf* was named by the Texas Library Association as one of five outstanding books for the Texas Sesquicentennial in 1986.

Kelton's work was full of humanity and treated all races, all ethnicities, women as well as men, with their deserved dignity as individuals. Their grace under pressure of undeserved discrimination is evident. And Crane citizens are justifiably proud of his Crane background.

---

34 **Affirmative Action.** Employment programs required by federal statutes and regulations designed to remedy discriminatory practices in hiring minority group members; https://en.wikipedia.org/wiki/Affirmative_action

35 Fort Davis was a post-Civil War US Army outpost now operated as a national park adjacent to the town of Fort Davis, in western Texas. It was occupied by regiments of black soldiers with white officers.

36 A note about the ever-present inequities: My daughter, just three years after this experience of Louie's, had a similar experience while practice teaching in Austin. A teacher left in the middle of the semester, and she was hired at a *regular teacher's pay* to finish the year in his place.

37 Elmer Kelton, *Wagontongue* (Fort Worth, Texas: Christian Universithy Press, 1972).

38 Elmer Kelton, *The Wolf and the Buffalo* (Garden City, NY: Doubleday & Co., Inc., 1986).

READER'S NOTES

There is no trickier subject for a writer from the South than that of affection between a black person and a white one in the unequal world of segregation. For the dishonesty upon which such a society is founded makes every emotion suspect, makes it impossible to know whether what flowed between two people was honest feeling or pity or pragmatism. Indeed, for the black person, the feigning of an expected emotion could be the very coinage of survival.
—Howell Raines, "Grady's Gift"[39]

Chapter 9

UNIVERSAL PERPLEXITIES

Much is made here of the uniqueness of our town's and each community's integration experience, and yet a look across the South reveals almost uncanny likenesses among whites of the segregated population. Recalling black and white friendships/relationships of the segregated yore calls up the same confusions, questions, even pain in many different settings.

To show how universal are our feelings and their evolvement, we'll first visit the grown-up children of three families widely separated in place and decades in the mid-twentieth century as they reflect on those days in this twenty-first century. We'll look into two families whose humanity compelled them totally to reverse their prejudices.

In the big picture of segregation/integration, one virtual group—individuals but termed a group here because they have so much in common—has some of the most difficulty in dealing with their remembered youthful relationships. They are the grown-up children of families who maintained an almost antebellum arrangement with their black household helpers.

Memories of childhood times now take on a painful character as they try to understand what was really happening with those black people, so beloved yet accepted as mere fixtures of their lives. These adults now read about race relations, talk about their own, and write about them, yet come to a dead end with unanswerable questions about this inexplicable and peculiarly American human condition.

I first became aware of such pain and perplexities as I visited with Sue Neeley Christon about her Crane childhood of the forties. Our friendship began when Bissinger's book focused some public attention on our Wall between the Races, and she spent a great deal of time here, in the town where she had grown up, seemingly obsessed with clearing her father from any reputation of racism. Because I understand obsessiveness all too well, I have tried to stand back and yet admonish her objectively/empathetically that she had nothing to prove, that *all* of us whites behaved a certain way toward blacks, in deference to the system, regardless of our personal feelings toward and relationships with blacks. Not one of us can point a finger at another, because that's the way it was. Period.

Then we talked about another aspect: Sue's relationship with her beloved Mable Williams, the black helper in her parents' hotel who was also a personal caretaker of the child Sue. I loved hearing about Mable almost as much as Sue loved telling about this lovable person who was more influential on Sue's behavior and thinking even than Sue's parents, how Mable carefully guarded the child's outlook, how Sue loved talking with Mable, and how she longed to spend more time in Mable's world, where the laughter and friendliness were so warm.

Then similar experiences and relationships popped up from everywhere—from Jackson, from Birmingham, from a farm in Stamford, Texas, and from my own childhood in Corpus Christi. As I read and heard reflections—painful reflections—from everywhere, it dawned how universal were these feelings.

Stockett

In the afterword to Kathryn Stockett's *The Help*, she introduced me to Howell Raines and his Pulitzer-prize-winning "Grady's Gift," wherein I found some of the same feelings expressed—sometimes in the same phrases—as Sue's and Stockett's. Then in letters from friends on the same subject, I was struck by the similarities of such experiences and of recollections with their accompanying feelings.[40]

Yes, it is a tricky matter and still defies illumination. As Aggies in my family say about their school's mystique: from the inside you can't explain it; from the outside you can't understand it. I did not attend Texas A&M, but I have an idea what they mean.

Still, they try—children of the forties and fifties and sixties, even seventies—to understand and explain. There seems an inherited guilt and yet a denial and even resentment of the guilt because they didn't ask for it. As children who did what they were told but could not—saw no need to—stifle their intellect, they were more perceptive than the adults of their day, or even the children themselves, guessed at the time.

Christon

Born in Crane in 1938, Sue Neeley Christon was a baby when Mable Williams came into her life. Much of her story of growing up at the busy business hub of town is told earlier in this work. Though she declares she is "not a writer," she was persuaded to write her history in words and pictures for the local museum. In the unpublished booklet she calls *My Times*, she has contributed a wealth of local historical information on both her parents' families, what brought them west by the scores (or maybe it just became scores after several met and married and had their own families), and what they did after they came.[41]

In doing so, she found what so many of my students have found—that writing things down helps the mind to organize and deal with such things. Writing, like talking, becomes cathartic. So, I believe, have many others found in dealing with such sentiments.

Sue now lives in Stanton, Texas, just a couple of hours away, but visits often in Crane to see friends and relatives and to inquire and talk about her Crane of old. She seems never to have quit worrying about righting the record of her daddy and his relationships—the whole family's relationships—with blacks, especially the Bill Hollins and Mable Williams families. She worries about her daddy's being forever labeled a racist because he built, or had built, the wall.

Upon reading Katherine Stockett's *The Help* and its afterword, "Too Little, Too Late," I was struck by the similarity of these two women's reflections. One a child of two hardworking parents in a hotel center of a young, busy, dusty western town, and one in a laid-back, tradition-steeped southern city home, they shared the same ponderings about their relationships with well-loved black caretakers.

Then, after Stockett's afterword introduced me to Howell Raines and his "Grady's Gift," the commonality of all their emotional reflections became huge. Here was this man whose childhood had been in a different decade in a different southern city, expressing the same appreciation, the same wonder, in writing about this tricky subject.

Raines

Born in Birmingham, Alabama, in 1943, Howell Raines was Washington, DC, bureau chief for the *New York Times* when he was awarded the Pulitzer Prize for Feature Writing for "Grady's Gift," a narrative of his Alabama childhood with a focus on Grady, the family's black housekeeper. Grady helped teach the child Raines about the reality of racism in the segregated Birmingham of the 1950s.

Raines was a child of seven when Grady came to iron and clean and cook for eighteen dollars a week, and she stayed for seven years.

He said that everyone in his family came to accept what his father called the long talks Howell had with Grady.

Howell followed Grady around the house, with Grady talking as she did her chores, marking the boy with her vision.

That reality became the inspiration for *My Soul Is Rested,* his 1977 history of the civil rights movement.

At a reunion forty years after teenager Grady first came to the Raines household, she told him that she had been moved upon seeing his book in a library. His response was true to the trend of us all now to look back with amazement at our own omissions.

He was surprised that Grady had not instantly understood that she was the book's inspiration. "It is her book, really," he said. "She wrote it on my heart in the acres of afternoon."[42]

Born in 1969 in Jackson, Mississippi, Katherine Stockett lived in a seventies time surprisingly parallel to Sue's in the forties and fifties and Raines's in fifties and sixties. It was the puzzlingly unequal world of segregation, where a white child could be influenced by, protected and educated by, and dearly loved by a black person whose world was as foreign to the child as China or other geography-book places.

Now that long-needed changes have opened the subject, stories like Christon's and Raines's and Stockett's could fill volumes of their own. Sue has never lived more than a hundred miles east of Crane, but her musings, even agonies, give her a kinship with Alabamans and Mississippians and—who knows how many thousand others? As Sue's experience and viewpoint help knit the Crane chronicle, so do varying accounts of others elsewhere weave all southern Americans together.

Three decades, several lifestyles, and hundreds of miles apart, each wrote of regrets for sins of omission in not seeing, asking, or caring more about that faraway world in the next block or across town that housed people they loved.

One could put together an imaginary but believable conversation from the exact writings of these three, with changes only in function words. There is an almost uncanny duplication of thoughts and even words and phrases about those long-ago situations still so clear in their minds and psyches, especially the subjects of talking and learning, protecting and being protected, and other interdependence of sorts.

On Talking and Learning

"Mable and I talked—I can't tell you what about—more with feelings and implications than with specific words," Sue said.

"I was influenced by Mable more than any of the whites around me, even my parents. I loved her more than anyone else. I probably think and act more like her than anyone else. Part of this love came in the form of discipline, as she treated me like her own, I thought."

Raines described many conversations with Grady as he followed her around while she worked.

"She spoke of a hidden world," he said, "in the midst of what Alabama novelist Babs Deal called the 'acres of afternoon,' those legendary hours of buzzing heat and torpidity that either bind you to the South or make you crazy to leave it—the world of 'nigger town.'

"She had been 'our maid,' but she taught me [a most] valuable lesson, to try to see—honestly and down to its very center—the world in which we live."

That was Grady's gift.

On Comfort and Watch Care—Both Ways

"Mabel was very protective of me," Sue said. "I was right in her footsteps a lot of times, and there were things in that hotel that she protected me from because it was full of men, and there were things in men's rooms that little girls shouldn't see. One room I could never could go into until Mabel went first, and of course that just increased my curiosity about that room."

When Sue was a little older and noticed a time when Mable was not around, she went up to the room by herself:

This man had ugly pictures all over his mirror. Mabel had put those in the drawer each time before she let me go in.

I can only speak from a view of a very loved and protected child in a world of her own. Part of this protection (from how things really were and how people really felt and what was really going on) came from Mable. She was mine. I can't tell you where this feeling came from, but Mable was from the old way. As whites would say, she knew her place. For example, she would eat with me but she would not sit down at the table to eat with Mother and Daddy even though she was asked to at times.

I loved to go to Mable's house and to the Dew-Drop Inn. I loved Mable's world, the feelings, the laughter. I always wanted to stay all night at her house, but she wouldn't let me. I was not a part of this world, but I didn't know it.

Stockett said that her caretaker Demetrie, at age twenty-eight, had come to cook and clean for the family when Kathryn's father was fourteen. By the time Kathryn knew her, Demetrie was married to a mean, abusive drinker. She wouldn't answer questions about him, but besides that subject, she'd talk to the children all day.

Kathryn loved sitting in her grandmother's kitchen, listening to Demetrie's stories and watching her mix up cakes and fry chicken, some of her outstanding cooking.

"It was something people discussed at length when they ate at my grandmother's table," Stockett said. "You felt *loved* when you tasted Demetrie's caramel cake."

She also felt loved when she took refuge in Demetrie's lap during times of childhood frustration.   Raines told of a reverse kind of protection: His brother, Jerry, was Grady's confidante and protector. They never spoke of it at the time, but she looked to him as her guardian against the neighborhood workmen of both races who were always eager to offer young black girls "a ride home from work."

"Even if it [wasn't true], Grady recalled to Raines, Jerry would always say, 'I'm going that way. I'll drop Grady off.'"

Years later, Raines wrote that he realized that his memory of Grady as "his" was a narrow and selfish child's memory. Grady also had bonds with Howell's siblings.

> Now I realize that we were both children—one white and very young, one black and adolescent; one privileged, one poor. The connection between these two children was [that] Grady saw to it that although I was to live in Birmingham for the first 28 years of my life, Birmingham would not live in me.
>
> We grew up in the '50s in that vanished world, two people who lived mundane, inconsequential lives while Martin Luther King, Jr., and Police Commissioner Eugene (Bull) Connor prepared for their epic struggle.

On Feelings

Sue said, "I want to ask black friends a question: how many whites knew how you really felt and what you really thought? You never let the whites into your world. I think this is even true today. How many would sit down and talk with a white person and share your true feelings, be a black brother? Does this come from generations of fear and hate?"

Undoubtedly so, Sue. As Raines has said, black people often had to feign emotions for survival's sake. Remember that in *The Help* one black maid could say nothing but "yes'm" when asked whether she liked her separate restroom. She would surely have disrupted her life had she told how she really felt.

And if Mable had sat down to eat with Sue's parents, what might have been a hurtful reaction from some of the hotel guests?

Grady's situation with the Raines family was a little different. She did reveal many feelings to her young master Howell about how bad it was to be black in her time and place, and in doing so she opened that door for him.

Stockett said she was pretty sure that no one in the family ever asked Demetrie what it felt like to be black in Mississippi, working for their white family. It never occurred to them to ask, she said.

"It was everyday life. It wasn't something people felt compelled to examine."

Not white people, anyway.

Closure

Though a popular word for coming to terms with the past, closure is a weak one here. For Christon, Raines, Stockett, and so many more of their kind, there will never be enough answers to pin down or tie up—to close—the subject.

Sue probably came closest. She was married with four young children when she and the family of six found and visited with Mable in Little Rock, Arkansas. They had made reservations at a nearby motel, but Mable would have none of that.

She had married well and had a big house.

"Soon after we got there," Sue said, "Mable started putting those babies to bed."

Then they all talked and talked.

So Sue finally got to spend the night at her Mable's home.

Raines too found Grady after their lives had changed.

After word that he had found Grady spread through his family, he worried because Grady remembered his mother as someone who had nagged her about the housework. But he found no one enjoyed the reunion more than Grady and his mother.

"My mother was disarmed," he said. "In the midst of a round of stories about the bold things Grady had said and done, I heard her explain to a visitor, 'You see, now, that Grady is a strong person.'"

What he sensed at the reunion, among his family, was something much deeper than fondness or nostalgia. It was a shared pride that in the Birmingham of the fifties this astonishing person had inhabited their home and had been allowed to be fully herself.

Grady was just another teenager in the house, he told, where there were already two teenagers, Howell's older siblings.

Stockett fared not so well.

Demetrie was long gone when Stockett was writing *The Help*.

"I have wished for many years," Stockett said, "that I'd been old enough and thoughtful enough to ask Demetrie that question. She died when I was sixteen. I've spent years imagining what her answer would be. And that is why I wrote this book."

So Stockett let her own characters do the asking and answering. A reader of *The Help* can see Stockton reliving vicariously as the young journalist who does ask the questions and write about the answers to the eventual improvement of many lives.

Perhaps that is why her main character in *The Help* felt devastated and helpless when she learned that her beloved black caretaker was long gone, unreachable and then dead before she thought to express appreciation. The woman who had stood a little girl who felt left out before a mirror and told her she was beautiful made a lifelong difference in the little girl's future. But the little girl didn't know it until she became a woman and looked back, like so many of us, with astonishment at our insensitivity in those days.

Conversations with friends have turned up literally dozens of similar stories, including my own. It's as if we all had the memories and the wonder and the vague guilt deep within us but didn't know what to do with it, couldn't fit it into our other interpersonal relationships, so didn't talk about it.

Until, as we have noted, bolder people risked their reputations and sometimes physical safety to make us see that blacks are people, not fixtures. Living, breathing beings, not puppets or pets.

THE WALL THAT FAILED

My Annie Mae

Annie Mae, a black woman who cleaned house and babysat us when my much-younger brothers were babies, was cheerful and fun. I don't remember any long conversations, but there was a little good-natured banter when she reminded me of something I was or wasn't supposed to do while Mother was gone. But I now see that I knew little and cared nothing that Annie was a person apart from us. I never wondered or asked anything about her family. Maybe my parents did, but I don't recall their saying anything to me about it. She was, I am ashamed to say, just an occasional fixture. Our home was never like Raines's and Stockett's: both my parents worked almost full-time in Daddy's store, and we were not affluent, so Annie Mae was not full-time.

Myriads of people my age have expressed some of the same thoughts, I'm sure. Friends I have asked nearly all have stories. Like Cris Grounds, a fellow teacher for many years, who grew up on a farm in Jones County, Texas, and returned there after retirement. Her comments echo Stockett's and many others'.

Cris's Virginia

"Virginia Wooten was black, her skin lighter than most, and she wore a braid on each side of her head that crossed over her crown," Cris wrote from Abilene. "She always wore a freshly starched apron, was always neat, had a smile on her face, and sang hymns as she worked.

"Once a week Mom would drive into town to pick her up to help in the garden or to clean house. She loved the corn season and Mom often sent an armful of food for her to take home. Mom always said that to be a good cook, you have to love cooking and not be stingy. That made for a great relationship between the two, who often worked together in the kitchen.

"I remember going to her house with Mom to pick up ironing occasionally. That was always exciting to me because she lived in

'The Flats,' called so because when it rained, water would stand on the flat land and make the streets muddy and driving almost impossible. From the car I could tell the yard was plain but neat, and black children would be playing and laughing in the street.

"As she grew older, she slowed down and had a little shuffle in her step. No matter how she felt, when Mom called her, she was happy to oblige. She and Mom sort of grew old together. My girls enjoyed seeing her in the summertime when we went to visit my parents. She always had a smile and hug for them. Now Mom and Virginia are both gone, and there are so many unanswered questions I wish I had asked. It makes me sad that I took her for granted all those years. Mom and my brother's family gave her a surprise birthday party one year, but since I was teaching and living some distance away, I didn't attend. I have lived to regret that decision.

"Because of her example of hard work, honesty, and loyalty, I know her children must have had a better life than she. I wish I could thank her for all those years she gave so unselfishly to my family, and who knows, some day that just might be possible."[43]

Yes, that inexplicable and peculiarly American human condition remains in a fog that we'll never clear on this earth. Still we try, and our efforts are a testimony to the unconscious and purely natural influence one human being of any color can have on another, and how love can thrive in its own bubble apart from the rest of society.

---

39 Howell Raines, "Grady's Gift," *New York Times*, December 1, 1991.
40 Kathryn Stockett, *The Help* (New York: Berkely Publishing Group, Penguin Group (USA) Inc., 2009).
41 S. N. Christon, *My Times,* 2013.
42 Howell Raines, "Grady's Gift," *New York Times*, December 01, 1991
43 Cristena Grounds, e-mail letter.

READER'S NOTES

IV
OUTLOOKS

Sure, some wall fragments physical and abstract remain, but we're working on it.

Has it come to your attention how the race of man
Has been climbing upward since time began,
How it's been climbing steady, and it's climbing there still,
But every time you notice it, it's going down hill?

★★★★★★★★★★★★★★

Going down hill is the way things run,
For the old have illusions and the young have fun,
And our manners and religions everlastingly decay,
Yet astonishing improvement is discernible today!
Hi-yo, Hi-yo, discernible today!

—Maxwell Anderson[44]

Chapter 10

UP A ROAD SLOWLY

"W<small>E NEED THIS MARKER TO REMIND</small> us of how far we've come," I said at the wall marker dedication, "and also how far we have to go."

Those of us who lived before and during integration may not need reminders, but many younger folks don't have a clue to what they see as "the olden days." Black and white young people are often aghast!

"Why would anyone do that?"

Who can say? Not I. It was just something that happened quietly, all along, even after integration, after great sports success, and so on. So when we zero in on any given time, we find instances of "going downhill." When we look at later homecoming dances, the kind of rejection Terry received isn't happening, but other things, such as swimming pool segregation and the like, are. Again, we look around today: swimming pools are integrated—actually, no one calls them integrated or not, as they're just swimming pools. Likewise schools, clubs, and most civic governing boards. And still we have a long way to go.

When the fact of integration came about, it did not automatically ensure that everyone would be treated fairly and equitably, would have his or her chance to be a regular citizen based on his character and actions, not on ancestry or color of skin. There were still the defensives, the belligerents, the discriminators, on the white *and* black sides.

After Crane schools were finally integrated, in 1966, we still had:

— The white teacher who tried to prove what he had said openly in biology class, that blacks were lazy.
— The man who got all kinds of flak—and possibly lost an election—for renting a house in a "white neighborhood" to a black family.
— The commissioner who said swimming pools could not be integrated because it would offend the oil companies and affect community economy.
— The highway crowd who repeatedly used the N word before the young black woman trying to do her civic duty.

THE WALL THAT FAILED

These incidents have been told earlier, but they keep turning up years later:

- a black student at CHS in the 90s was berated by a black classmate for taking the role of the black maid in a classic play. She and I agreed that some people didn't understand what acting is.
- the drive-in attendants who would not serve a group of driver education students because they saw a black student in the car.

Louie Jones, friendly and fun-loving enough to find no problems with black *or* white kids, had been in the integrated Crane schools several years when that incident happened. He and other driver education students were taking turns driving with teacher Arlen White one summer afternoon when they stopped at a drive-in in a nearby town. After waiting "quite a while" to be served, White put a head and arm out the window to signal a carhop—or whatever we call them now. But the person who responded just nodded toward Louie and said that she could not serve him.

"I—I didn't know what to do," Louie told me years later, with that puzzled little-boy look, "but Coach White took care of it; he just looked disgusted and pulled out to go to another place for our drinks." I know Arlen well and can imagine the look was the same almost amused/scornful "What's the matter with you?" look that had told a few students through the years when they were way off base.

So how did we get here from there? At the base of this road that usually seems to be going downhill is a foundation: we Americans have a *Constitution*. It was the world's first document of its kind and contains principles that even some of its composers ignored, reinterpreted, and generally pushed around.

Likewise, the constitution's earlier born sibling, the *Declaration of Independence*. Had that first statement by the united colonies been the way Thomas Jefferson (a slave owner himself) originally penned it, we might have gone down the road a little faster on some things. But—bless his visionary heart—Jefferson knew that an unpassed

Declaration would help no one, so he tweaked it a little to make it more inclusive of the slave states. He took out, as one complaint against King George, that sovereign's encouragement of the slave trade.

At that time, slaves were little more than half persons, three-fifths actually in counting population for purposes of representation. They didn't do any fraction of the voting, though, and neither did white women, though they were counted as whole people for representation. So males of white/European origin, though fewer than half the human beings in the new country, were essentially designated to represent all the rest. Not much of a democracy, some might say, but one of those steps that leads upward even while we're going downhill.

Not much of a democracy, some might say of the Magna Charta signed by King John of England in 1215. Though the common man seems to have gained nothing from these rights wrested from the king, this guarantee to the barons was, in the big picture, the first step of individual freedom *under law*, not under a person.

So it is easy to believe that the freedom-loving but pragmatic men who laid our bedrock, our constitution, knew exactly how to walk at the edge of aristocracy while providing the language framework for more democratic interpretations than most leaders of the day could make. It was, some might say, providential. They were just men, many slaveholders themselves, all of privileged class, but in carving this plan for the new country, they seem all to have revered principles over entitlements, if just barely.

We'll never make most young people believe it—I wouldn't have at their age—but there are, as a slightly younger friend said recently, some great things about getting older. We can look back down our road and see that some "astonishing improvement is discernible today."

We can also see that where we've been must be a factor in knowing where we're going and how. That's why we who see that big picture must preserve some things.

THE WALL THAT FAILED

So we marked our Wall between the Races for reasons similar to those that inspired "Never Again," written on the walls of the former prison—now a monument—at Dachau, Germany. Some events must be remembered that we not let them be repeated, must be admitted that we continue to distance ourselves from them.

And here is my subjective reminder for this chapter. I feel no guilt for what my ancestors did, any more than I blame anyone for injustices *to* my ancestors. During World War II, my little German grandmother, who didn't know that her husband's being a naturalized citizen of the United States didn't make her one, had to be monitored by the Alien and Sedition Board. She was five feet tall and was afraid of thunderstorms and lightning, but she was not allowed to keep even a camera—and of course not a gun—in her house. And any time she came to Corpus Christi to visit us, she had to call the A&S office in Houston, where she lived, and get permission to be out of town for a designated time.

It sounds almost cruel now, but what else could our country do? I am also told that in Sealy, Texas, where my father grew up and where some relatives still live, the largely German-speaking population were very careful to use English or not speak at all when a stranger came through town.

But back to our racial bias today, there's a little guilt/regret within me that I did not take a more active part in protesting segregation when I knew deep down how inhumane it was. But that is what made me and others in my generation so ready to do our part in making integration work when it came to us.

That syndrome—getting on the bandwagon eagerly when we were officially required to—seems pretty universal across the Texas and the South. After the sixties, we saw some well-known figures who once stood firmly, even pugnaciously, against integration, "coming 'round" to express remorse, even to apologize, for their previous actions.

But maybe more importantly, we have seen many groups beyond school teachers who hastened to do the right thing, even admitting that it was a little late. My sphere of action/observation is pretty limited, but I did see Texas officials do what they could to make up for virtually ignoring black school sports for years, and I "lived" for several summers very close to an old-style family in Mississippi who, when change was forced upon them, also made a voluntary change in attitude.

Accomplishments of our black athletes, namely basketball players, in preintegration days has been told earlier in this book. But though a number of local whites, mostly men, enjoyed the Bethune games, the black school's accomplishments—even state championships—received no community acclaim other than verbal comments and a small story in the weekly paper. Certainly there was nothing from Austin to compare with the recognition CHS received, including a visit from the UIL director, when winning the state academic meet once (never an athletic team championship).

But in the 1970s some powers that be woke up to black athletes throughout the state and made an effort to extend a retroactive recognition they surely knew they should have made all along. They invited winning teams from all over the state to Austin for a rousing recognition. Bethune players finally had their statewide acclaim. Cookie's leaflets from that event we copied and put in the museum.

The personal level change I witnessed in Mississippi makes an even more lasting impression. Because my husband's parents spent over a decade in the state (transplanted there with an oil company), our family spent the better part of several summers with them. They lived in a small neighborhood (had once been a community with a train stop) a few miles through the pine forest from a very small town a few miles out from Natchez. They rented an old, roomy house across the road from the "big house" that looked and operated for all the world like an old-style plantation house.

When the man of the family (I'll call him Ed here) came in from town, he blew his horn as he passed by the houses of black families, and that meant someone—usually one of the children—was to come down to help him unload whatever he had brought from town. Black people worked the white family's flower beds and kitchen garden, washed their clothes, came at their beck and call for whatever.

THE WALL THAT FAILED

A black maid who had a large family of her own did the cooking for that family in the big house, another for my in-laws. They were paid, of course, but not much. Most of the black and white families had known one another for generations, and there was an easy comradeship among them. Their children sometimes came down to play with our children.

But nearly every feature of life there was reminiscent of slave days, even to the long, winding road traveled through the pines to get there.

"Watch out for those log trucks," my father-in-law said every time anyone ventured to town or back. One needed to watch out, all right, as the trucks were a regular feature. Our friends in the big house made part of their living, like some other families down deeper into the woods, from selling lumber.

Then came the seventies. Charles's parents had retired and returned to Texas, some of the Hartes had died and some had moved to the small town, and now we visited them in their home there, as their friendship had become closer than kin in some ways.

Integration was, in spite of many setbacks, finally a grudging reality in Mississippi. Many places, like the town where our friends lived, had their own "legal" form of resistance. They were establishing a private school, and fundraising was a busy-ness there. Imagine our surprise when Ed said there were to be no cakes baked in his home for the sale or other support for that private school. They had given their loyal maid a car, and she drove into town nearly every day to work for them, and Ed said for them to support this school would be offensive to her and her family.

One of Ed's coffee-drinking buddies, of his same generation, also surprised me when he said, "They call it a County Christian School, but it's built on hate and prejudice."

Amazing. This from a man who just a few years earlier had been benignly kind enough to blacks but demanded they "stay in their place," and that did not include mingling with white children in school or church. Maybe he and Ed and many others had been waiting for the law to let them do what they knew they needed to do all along, just like the teachers I often refer to.

The last time we visited these Mississippi folks, we drove out—through the pines again, but the road was somewhat widened—to see the old places. The loyal maid now lived in the Hartes' old family place. Her grandson, now a teacher, was washing his car in front of that house. He remembered us from the days when he used to help Mr. Ed bring in his groceries and the like from town. Along with a nostalgia for the times that had been, I had to rejoice at the new times that are.

Another example of white folks "coming 'round" comes from westward. A cousin in New Mexico had a lifelong typical attitude: he was a kind man in his behavior toward anyone but was quick and easy on the draw if anyone started a conversation about racial equality/integration. I took a wonderful book, *The Color of Water*[45], to their home. Jim's wife read it, but Jim would not touch it after I explained that it was the story of a Jewish woman who had married a black man, a story told by their son.

"Thanks," he said, "but I don't believe in that and don't want to know or discuss anything about it."

Jim had lived, optimistically and enthusiastically, with a bad heart for years, but came the day we all knew it was playing out. Hospice sent him—of all the ironies—a black minister. At first Jim was polite but cool, but I was blessed to be at his home for a wonderful scene. The black minister was visiting, and several of us were talking in Jim's bedroom when Jim broke a short silence.

"Brother—I want you to know something." There was a pause, and then he said, "When I was younger, I was very prejudiced, and I am so sorry now."

His voice broke then, but there was no need to say more.

"Well, Brother Jim," said the minister, "don't you know that Peter had the same problem, and God took care of it, just like he's taking care of yours, now."

That soft voice and tears in Jim's eyes are impressed in my memory forever.

Some fragments of that wall—concrete and abstract, positive and negative—remain, to remind us of where we've been and where we're going.

And there's still plenty each of us can do now to move up that road a little faster.

---

44 Maxwell Anderson, "Hi-yo, Hi-yo, Discernible Today (A Song after Reading Toynbee)," *New Yorker* (May 1, 1948): 26.
45 James McBride, *The Color of Water: A Blak Man's Tribute to His White Mother,* New York: Riverhead Books, 1996.

READER'S NOTES

Who knoweth whether thou art come to the kingdom for such a time as this?
—Esther 4:14 KJV

AFTERWORD

So we come full circle. After the dedication to Tommy Jones of the gym in which he never played, hordes of people who played with him, who played against him, and who watched him—some coming from miles around—continue to celebrate this remarkable person. Likewise his teachers and classmates beyond fellow athletes.

Tommy's family who haven't lived in Crane—this is the first time for many of us to meet his wife, Pat—are amazed at the many accomplishments this guy had never told them about. We who knew him in school are not surprised that the same gentle modesty Tommy had when he came to CHS as a freshman, before his talents came to acclaim in the black *and* white world, was still a part of him in later life.

Tommy stories of all kinds abound. Particularly of his graciousness, his humor, and a gentleness that almost belied the ferocity with which he could charge forward and run roughshod in athletics.

Jack Gothard, coach of that 1967 team that went to state the first year of integration, beams to tell how the Bethune boys had inspired others to be their best.

Arlen White's voice cracks as he speaks of Tommy's deep faith evident in his conversations.

And in the halls and the student union room before and after the program, many of his fellow players and other classmates, teachers and other friends, wearing purple basketball pins made by the Jones family, are in groups exchanging Tommy stories with similar themes.

Dexter Tooke, a bike-a-thon athlete with his own fame, echoes what many say of being privileged to play with this player's player, an all-class gentleman who drew admiration of competitors as well as teammates.

Henry Anderson, Crane coach who grew up in McCamey, tells of challenges in playing against Tommy. One student tells of a racial slur from the opposing fans, shrugged off by Tommy, who signaled his teammates to do the same,

Not that the sixties era in Crane, like anything else told in this chronicle, was perfect. Not that anyone, present company not excepted, was perfect. There were of course negatives, common to high school athletics. One student tells of a racial slur from the opposing fans, shrugged off by Tommy, who signaled his teammates to do the same. And we hear even of an occasional teammate who tried a little more for his own glory and perhaps cost the team some points by not passing the ball, but those things fade away as the light of teamwork and camaraderie of the sixties grows brighter with time. There could even be some negatives about Tommy—nobody's perfect—but not tonight.

I recalled Bobby Tillman's e-mail comment when he realized he wouldn't get to the gym dedication.

> I had a long conversation with Tommy at our 30th class reunion. He said he was a motivational speaker. He said he never [gave up but one time]. During the Crane vs Big Lake [football] game, when Crame ranked #1 and Big Lake #2 in State, Jojo Barnes did a QB sneak on 4th and 1 from the 30. I think the score was Crane 6 and BL 6 at that point. Jojo was running for a TD and Tommy was chasing him. But Tommy quit running when he was clipped, thinking the play would be called back. But it wasn't, and there 30 years later he was telling me that was the only time he gave up in his life. Great story.

THE WALL THAT FAILED

Bobby loved the subject and told more about his and Tommy's senior year.

> Well, Gary McCarron and I have talked about how watching him we knew he was good but in the Crane element, I don't think we knew how good. It was an expectation then. Gary Mc and I went to every home basketball game our senior year. In a game against AAA Andrews [Crane was AA], at the end of the first quarter it was Crane 38 Andrews 0. All Tommy.
>
> Gary Mc's dad drove us to another district away game, and that was our only district loss. There was some real home cookin' going on—I probably understand home cookin' and racism now, but I didn't understand that then. One opposing player jammed Tommy into the wall on a layup late, and fans swarmed the court. The other player's mama ran down to protect him. Sitting on the second row, we were warned about a technical after we threw all sorts of paper on the court.
>
> Gary Mc and I rode one of four student buses to Austin for the Championship Tourney. I still remember the FW Kirkpatrick game. Tommy was fouled on the final play of the game, trailing by 3. He went out and sunk both free throws and we lost by 1.
>
> They took us back to Crane and we missed the consolation game. Crane lost that too.

We watch films of the '67 state playoff game—silent, of course, but we still hear the roaring standing ovation the Cranes received even as they lost this final playoff game to become second in state AAA, that first year of our integration.

Eventually we have to say good night, it's been great to see you, and let's stay in touch. Tommy's family promises to come back next year for this same tournament. I think they will. And I know this story is not done but at a pausing place.

Yes, we've come full circle, and now it's time to spin off that circle, into a future that makes the best of what we see here tonight. As we celebrate how far we've come, we take hope for the future—the same hope and plea Langston Hughes spoke of in "Let America Be America Again."

We could say the "dream the dreamers dreamed," as Hughes put it, is in the soul of the US Constitution. There "life, liberty, and the pursuit of happiness" are set as the goal for all men, where the founders advisedly used the word "men" in the biblical sense—"male and female created He them" with no color specification.

Though the Constitution framers made no provision for women to vote, though they counted slaves as three-fifths a person each for representation purposes, these items and other matter-of-course procedures were still under the "created equal" umbrella when their dream country was mature enough to give women and blacks a closer look—as people, as mankind, male and female.

Hughes speaks, he pleads, and yearns—for the immigrant full of hope, the farmer bound to the soil, the Negro servant, the pioneer, all who believed the American dream—for return to that dream, held by the serfs who came from Europe, slaves torn from Africa. He wants and still declares possible the dream America used to be, though it has never has been that for him, never been America to him. What an inspiration this guy has been in his poetry that continues to live after him.

THE WALL THAT FAILED

We must take back our land again,
America!

America never was America to me,
And yet I swear this oath—
America will be!

We, the people, must redeem
The land, the mines, the plants, the rivers.
The mountains and the endless plain—
and make America America again![46]

---

46 Langston Hughes, "Let America Be America Again."

AFTER-AFTERWORD

It's happened again.

Just when this story is about to go out comes an event that must be included.

At the Tommy Jones celebration, it seemed so clear we had come to the milestone that would make a fitting stopping place for this never-ending story. But always there was yet another interview, another contact with a printer and so on until, nearly two years after the T. Jones event, comes the delight of yet another milestone.

Full circle indeed.

September 21, 2013—Jack Lane, father of the fourteen Lane children now all grown up as good citizens, is honored as Heritage Day citizen of the year. To my knowledge, no black person has ever been so recognized in this or any area town.

This was the seventh Heritage Day celebration, sponsored by the chamber of commerce to recognize the town's history and the people who helped build it. Its first recognition was of Paul Patterson, a teacher/writer/humorist of some local note from even before Crane was a town.

As last year's recipient, I had the privilege of going with Betty Damron, Historical Commission chairman and member of the chamber, to Jack's home in August to announce his selection. Children, grandchildren, in-laws, and a few great-grands, having known what was coming, had "dropped in" on him to wait for our visit. And what a treat that was.

Daisy videoed the jig her father danced as the group sang "For He's a Jolly Good Fellow." Our date for an interview the next week had to be in the afternoon because he said he works—on cars, house, whatever—most mornings. At ninety years of age.

After the doctor said that work was keeping him alive and active, the children backed off asking him to stop.

But a few years ago, he sold his garage. Retirement? Not! He still does "some work" at home.

"It keeps me pretty busy keeping the children's and my friends' cars up, and that's a way I can save them some money."

His reputation as a good mechanic and his and (especially) his wife's reputation as firm disciplinarians were known to me long before I interviewed him. I taught eight of those children, taught school *with* two of them, taught several grandchildren, and so on—and teachers can usually tell something of parents from their children.

There's always more to this chronicle, and we're leaving some blank pages for owners of the book to add their own memories and new events and thoughts.

But this one had to be told, as an illustration of the spirit of love and fellowship among the races in Crane.

Not that all was smooth and easy. Not that there aren't events we wish had never happened, events to regret, but that we want to move on. No one I think wants that more than some of my black friends. Jack Lane is not the only one who said so. And then he told me of some of the good times with his family and friends, black and white.

As Tommy Jones was a prototype, a role model if you will, for gentle and congenial integration, the Lane family has been a prototype for making the best of life at every stage, believing in "blooming where one is planted."

A model for any family.

ABOVE: Faith in Christ church today, with cement base at left showing location of burned sanctuary; ABOVE RIGHT: Jack Lane with son Ellis standing on exact spot (front right in church picture) where young family lived when they first came to Crane (Photo by Daisy/Cookie Lane)

Lane home today (two-story house with carport behind four large trees), built first by Jack and rebuilt after burning with community help.

APPENDICES

January 2, 1947: Bill of sale of West 5.089 acres of development tract by Neeleys to Don Hollins

LEON NEELEY, ET AL

TO

BILL HOLLINS

WARRANTY DEED

THE STATE OF TEXAS
COUNTY OF CRANE

KNOW ALL MEN BY THESE PRESENTS:

That we, Leon Neeley and wife Edna Neeley and J. V. Neeley and wife Ethel Neeley of the County of Crane and State of Texas, for and in consideration of the sum of Five Hundred Eight and no/100 Dollars to us in hand paid by Bill Hollins, the receipt of which is hereby acknowledged, have granted, sold and conveyed, and by these presents do grant, sell and convey, unto the said Bill Hollins of the County of Crane State of Texas, all that certain lot, tract or parcel of land situate and being in the County of Crane and State of Texas, and being the West 5.08 acres out of a 26 3/4 acre tract out of Section No. 40 Certificate No. 2044, W. A. Bates Original Grantee and being a part of a 26 3/4 acre tract conveyed by G. T. Hall and wife and A. D. Neal and wife to Leon Neeley and J. V. Neeley by deed dated December 28th, 1946, and described by metes and bounds as follows:

BEGINNING at a plunger coupling and rock mound in the East line of Section No. 7, Block X, C.C.S.D.&R.G.N.G. Ry. Co., and the Southwest corner of a 347.2 acre tract out of the North part of Survey No. 40, Certificate No. 2044, W. A. Bates for the Northwest corner of this tract;

THENCE North 74°30' East with the North line of said 26 3/4 acre tract 500 feet to a stake;

THENCE South 15°30' West 441.8 feet to the South line of said 26 3/4 acre tract, a stake;

THENCE South 74°30' West with the South line of said 26 3/4 acre tract 500 feet to a point in the East line of Section No. 7 Block X, whence the Southeast corner of said Section No. 7 Block X, bears South 15°30' East 1109 varas.

THENCE North 15°30' West 441.8 feet to the place of beginning.

Reserving from this grant the minerals as the same are reserved in the deed from G. T. Hall and wife and A. D. Neal and wife to Leon Neeley and J. V. Neeley, dated December 28th, 1946.

To have and to hold the above described premises, together with all and singular the rights and appurtenances thereto in anywise belonging, unto the said Bill Hollins and his heirs and assigns forever, and we do hereby bind ourselves and our heirs, executors and administrators, to WARRANT AND FOREVER DEFEND, all and singular, the said premises unto the said Bill Hollins and his heirs and assigns, against every person whomsoever lawfully claiming or to claim the same or any part thereof.

WITNESS our hands at Crane, Texas, this 2nd day of January, A.D. 1947 1949

LEON NEELEY
EDNA NEELEY
J. V. NEELEY
ETHEL NEELEY

THE STATE OF TEXAS
COUNTY OF CRANE

BEFORE ME, E. D. Smith, a Notary Public in and for Crane County, Texas, on this day personally appeared Leon Neeley known to me to be the person whose name is subscribed to the foregoing instrument, and acknowledged to me that he executed the same for the purposes and consideration therein expressed.

Given under my hand and seal of office, this 3rd day of January, A.D. 1947.

SEAL

E. D. Smith (E: D. Smith)
Notary Public, Crane County, Texas.

THE STATE OF TEXAS
COUNTY OF CRANE

February 3, 1947: Dedication deed of development now to be known as Park Addition to the city of Crane

LEON NEELEY, ET AL

TO

F. E. COVILL

AGREEMENT

THE STATE OF TEXAS
COUNTY OF CRANE

KNOW ALL MEN BY THESE PRESENTS:

That we, Leon Neeley and J. V. Neeley parties of the first part and F. E. Covill, party of the second part, both of Crane County, Texas, have this day made and entered into the following agreement, to-wit:

Party of the first part, for and in consideration of the sum of Ten and no/100 Dollars ($10.00) to them in hand paid by F. E. Covill, the receipt of which is hereby acknowledged, hereby agrees, binds and obligates themselves, their heirs, executors and administrators, to give and grant said party of the second part the option to buy and to convey to him by general warranty deed or to any person, persons or corporation he may designate, and to furnish and deliver to him a complete certified abstract of title to the date thereof, showing a good and merchantable title, at any time that said party of the second part may demand on or before the 1st day of February A.D. 1948, for the sum of One Hundred Fifty and no/100 Dollars ($150) to be paid to the said parties of the first part in cash for each separate lot described herein, and a deed for any one or more lots in one or several demands, within the term of this option, the following described tracts of land situated in Crane County, Texas, as follows:

All of Blocks No. Four (4), Five (5), Twelve (12) and Thirteen (13).
Lots No. One (1) and Two (2) in Block No. Six (6)
Lots No. One (1), Two (2), Three (3) and Four (4) in Block No. Eleven, (11);
Lots No. Three (3) and Four (4) in Block No. Three (3)
Lots No. Seven (7), Eight (8), Nine (9) and Ten (10) in Block No. Fourteen (14);
All in the PARK ADDITION TO THE CITY OF CRANE, as the same are shown on the plat of said addition filed in the office of the County Clerk of Crane County, Texas.

Said parties of the first part further agrees, binds and obligates themselves that they will not sell or encumber said real estate or any part thereof during the term of this option and in the event they should do so, they shall and will forfeit the sum of One Hundred Fifty and no/100 Dollars ($150.00) to the said party of the second part as liquidated damages. Failure or refusal by said parties of the first part to make and deliver a deed on any lot on demand made, or to furnish said abstract as above provided, they shall and will forfeit to said party of the second part as liquidated damages the sum of One Hundred Fifty and no/100 Dollars ($150.00). All claims for damages for failure to close this option are hereby waived by the parties of the first part.

This contract signed in duplicate originals, this the 1st day of February, A.D. 1947.

Leon Neeley
First Party

J. V. Neeley
First Party

F. E. Covill
Second Party

THE STATE OF TEXAS
COUNTY OF CRANE

BEFORE ME, the undersigned authority, on this day personally appeared Leon Neeley, J. V. Neeley and F. E. Covill all known to me to be the persons whose names are subscribed to the foregoing instrument and acknowledged to me that they each executed the same for the purposes and consideration therein expressed.

Given under my hand and seal of office, this the 3rd day of February A.D. 1947.

(SEAL)

E. D. Smith (E. D. Smith)
Notary Public, Crane County, Texas

April 29, 1947: Letter from FHA stating requirements
for FHA-insured housing (two pages)

NATIONAL HOUSING AGENCY

FEDERAL HOUSING ADMINISTRATION
District Director
Ft. Worth 2, Texas

April 29, 1947

Mr. F. E. Covill
Crane, Texas
      RE: Park Addition, Crane, Texas

Dear Sir:

In accordance with your request, we have made an inspection of this tract, described above, and have carefully analyzed your proposal with respect to the contemplated development of this project.

This office is prepared to entertain individual applications for mortgage insurance subject to the requirements and recommendations as set forth in this letter. The Federal Housing Administration, however, does not render opinions as to the eligibility of entire tracts, nor are subdivisions either approved or disapproved by this Agency.

We welcome the opportunity of being of service to you in this instance and are pleased to extend our advice and suggestions to you in the interests of a sound development program for this project.

While the entire contents of this letter are merely recommendations on our part, the following paragraphs, numbered from 1 to 16, inclusive, will be imposed as actual requirements, in the event applications for mortgage insurance are to be received relating to individual properties situated in this tract.

      MORTGAGE INSURANCE REQUIREMENTS:

1. The plat, in final form, showing complete and accurate dimensions of lots, setback lines, rights of way, public areas, easements and tract boundaries shall be recorded and three certified copies shall be furnished this office.

2. The proposed protective covenants covering all lots in the tract shall be submitted to this office for approval prior to recording. When finally accepted by this office, the protective covenants shall be recorded against the entire tract. Three certified copies of the recorded covenants shall be furnished this office.

3. Restrictive covenants finally accepted shall contain a clause that no lot shall ever be sub-divided in a building plot less than that shown on the plat-60' in width and all buildings shall face as the lot faces.

4. All lots in said addition, not controlled by sponsor, shall be restricted to residential construction with minimum square feet area similar to those imposed on these lots controlled by subject sponsor.

233

(second page of FHA letter above)

Page 2

RE: Park Addition, Crane, Texas

5. This office shall be furnished certified copies of all easement agreements, if any, right-of-way agreements, oil and mineral leases, and reservations affecting subject addition, if any, and they should be properly located in plat of said addition.

6. Any existing mortgages shall be subordinated to the Protective Covenants so that foreclosure will not void the covenants.

7. The streets shall be improved in accordance with the following:
   a. Provide a concrete curb per data sheet SJ-351.
   b. Streets shall be properly graded and paved with at least eight inches of compacted gravel from curb to curb.
   c. Acceptance by City of dedication of all streets in said addition by City Commissioners, Crane, Texas, for continuous maintenance without special maintenance lien being placed on the property.
   d. Improved to connect with all adjacent improved streets in accordance with the current specifications covering street improvements established by the City of Crane,
   e. Grading as per data sheet SG-101.
   f. Provided with proper grades to assure adequate surface and ground-water drainage.
   g. Street trees as per data sheet SO-101.
   h. Street name signs as per data sheet SQ-101.
   i. Sidewalks as per data sheet SN-101.

8. The following utilities shall be installed to serve the lots in a manner meeting local requirements and FHA Property Standards and shall be furnished to the improvements on each lot prior to insurance of mortgage.
   a. Natural gas
   b. Electricity
   c. City Sewer and Water
   d. Fire hydrants shall be spaced every 700 feet and shall be served with water mains not less than 6 inches in diameter.

9. All utility poles and lines shall be placed in alleys reserved for such purposes.

10. Yard grades shall be finished to at least six feet from the foundation walls to drain the surface water away from the house.

11. The entire yard shall be raked to remove clods and rocks and top soil shall be applied if necessary.

12. Shrubbery shall be planted in number, size and manner satisfactory to the FHA for each dwelling, a guarantee that same will live for one year or be replaced, shall be provided this office.

13. Developments shall be closely grouped and expanded in a fairly contiguous manner.

14. A nucleus of not less than five homes shall be constructed in subject addition before any mortgage is insured.

15. Definite assurance that negro homes two blocks southeast shall be moved and a letter from City Secretary that a new Negro section has been established shall be furnished this office.

16. This Administration reserves unto itself the right to withhold approval for the beginning of construction on any building site wherein the site grade and/or drainage facilities are not deemed satisfactory or adequate.

October 18, 1947: Letter from Crane to FHA office in Fort Worth about fulfilling FHA requirements

CITY OF CRANE

October 18, 1947.

Federal Housing Administration
District Director
Ft. Worth 2, Texas.

Dear Sir: Re: Park Addition, Crane, Texas.

    This is to confirm the meeting of requirements and conditions, insofar as they concern the City of Crane, set forth in a document dated April 29, 1947.

    Page 2 Section 8. Natural Gas, Electricity, City Sewer and Water has been installed. Fire Hydrants are spaced 700 feet or less on 8" water mains. Poles and lines are placed in the alleys.

    Page 2 Section 14. The Negro Section 2 blocks South East of the FHA Project has been moved.

    A Negro Section has been established elsewhere and all negro houses and families have been moved on to it.

Sincerely Yours,

A.N. Wright, City Supt.

October 22, 1947: Letter from Crane to FHA office, same as October 18 letter with addition of one paragraph

#5 FHA requirements

W.W. Allman

10-22-1947

October 22, 1947.

Federal Housing Administration
District Director
Fort Worth 2, Texas.

Gentlemen:

Re: Your letter of April 29, 1947
City of Crane Park Add. Requirements.

This is to confirm the meeting of requirements and conditions insofar as they concern the City of Crane, set forth in your letter of April 29, 1947.

Page 2 Section 7, c, d and f have been and will continue to meet the conditions.

Page 2 Section 8, Natural Gas, Electricity, City sewer and water has been installed. Fire Hydrants are spaced 700 feet or less apart on 8" water mains.

Page 2 Section 14. The Negro section 2 blocks South East of the FHA Project has been moved.

A Negro Section has been established elsewhere and all negro houses and families have been moved onto it.

The City Officials are anxious to meet all requirements they may be called upon to perform.

Sincerely yours,

A.N. Wright, City Supt.

December 6, 1947: Replat of Park Addition with deed restrictions (four pages)

LEON NEELEY, ET AL

TO

EX PARTE

INSTRUMENT: REPLAT

DATED : DECEMBER 6, 1947

FILED :

RECORDED : VOL. 50 PAGE 403
DEED RECORDS, CRANE COUNTY, TEXAS

STATE OF TEXAS
COUNTY OF CRANE

KNOW ALL MEN BY THESE PRESENTS

That we, J.V. Neeley and wife, Ethel Neeley, Leon Neeley and wife, Edna Neeley, James E. Covill and wife, Bonnie V. Covill, and F.E. Covill, a single man, being all of the owners of Blocks 3, 4, 5, 6, 11, 12, 13, 14, 19, 20, 21 and 22 in Park Addition to the City of Crane, Crane County, Texas, do hereby adopt the attached REPLAT of said Blocks and place the following restrictions upon said Blocks as covenants which are to run with the land and which shall be binding on all parties and all persons claiming under them until January 1, 1968, at which time said Covenants shall be automatically extended for successive periods of 10 years unless by vote of a majority of the then owners of the lots it is agreed to change said covenants in whole or in part.

If the parties hereto, or any of them, or their heirs or assigns, shall violate or attempt to violate any of the Covenants herein it shall be lawful for any other person or persons owning any real property situated in said development or subdivision to prosecute any proceedings at law or in equity against the person or persons violating or attempting to violate any such Covenant and either to prevent him or them from so doing to recover damages or other dues for such violation.

Invalidation of any one of these Covenants by judgment or court order shall in no wise affect any of the other provisions which shall remain in full force and effect.

All lots in said blocks shall be known and described as residential lots.

No structures shall be erected, altered, placed, or premitted to remain on any residential building plot other then one detached single-family dwelling or one semi-detached single-family dwelling not to exceed one and one-half stories in height and a private garage for not more than 2 cars and wash house or storage building.

No building shall be located nearer to the front lots line or nearer to the side street line than the building setback lines shown on the recorded plat. In any event, no building shall be located on any residential building plot nearer than 33 feet to the front lot line, nor nearer than 12 feet to any side street line. No building, except a detached garage or other outbuilding located 100 feet or more from the front lot line, shall be located nearer than five feet to any side lot line.

No residential structure shall be erected or placed on any building plot, which plot has an area of less then 7,000 square feet or a width of less than 60 feet at the front building setback line.

No noxious or offensive trade or activity shall be carried on upon any lot nor shall anything be done thereon which may be or become an annoyance or nuisance to the neighborhood.

No trailer, basement, tent, shack, garage, barn, or other outbuilding erected in the tract shall at any time be used as a residence temporatily or permanently, nor shall any structure of a temporary character be used as a residence.

No dwelling costing less than $2,500.00 shall be permitted on any lot in the tract. The ground floor area of the main structure, exclusive of one-story open proches and garages, shall not be less than 700 square feet in the case of a one-story structure nor less than 1050 square feet in the case of a one and one-half story structure

Witness our hands at Crane, Texas, December 6, 1947.

F.E.Covill	Bonnie V.Covill	Edna Neeley
James E.Covill	Leon Neeley	Ethel Neeley
		J.V.Neeley

STATE OF TEXAS

COUNTY OF CRANE

BEFORE ME, the undersigned, a Notary Public in and for said County and State, on this day personally appeared J.V.Neeley, Leon Neeley, James E.Covill, and F.E.Covill, known to me to be the persons whose names are subscribed to the foregoing instrument, and acknowledged to me that they executed the same for the purposes and consideration therein expressed, Given under my hand and seal of office this the 6 day of December, 1947.

(SEAL)   A.N.Wright   A.N.WRIGHT
           Notary Public in and for
           Crane County, Texas

STATE OF TEXAS

COUNTY OF CRANE

BEFORE ME, the undersigned, a Notary Public in and for said County and State, on this day personally appeared Ethel Neeley, wife of J.V.Neeley, known to me to be the person whose name is subscribed to the foregoing instrument, and having been examined by me privily and apart from her husband, and having the same fully explained to her, she, the said Ethel Neeley acknowledged such instrument to be her act and deed and she declared that she had willingly signed the same for the purposes and consideration therein expressed, and that she did not wish to retract it. Given under my hand and seal of office this the 6 day of December, 1947.

(SEAL)   A.N.Wright   A.N.WRIGHT
           Notary Public in and for
           Crane County, Texas

STATE OF TEXAS

COUNTY OF CRANE

BEFORE ME, the undersigned, a Notary Public in and for said County and State, on this day personally appeared Edna Neeley, wife of Leon Neeley, knwon to me to be the person whose name is subscribed to the foregoing instrument, and having the same fully explained to her and having been examined by me privily and apart from her husband, she, the said Edna Neeley acknowledged such instrument to be her act and deed, and she declared that she had willingly signed the same for the purposes and consideration therein expressed, and that she did not wish to retract it. Given under my hand and seal of office this the 6 day of December, 1947.

(SEAL)   A.N.Wright   A.N.WRIGHT
           Notary Public in and for
           Crane County, Texas

STATE OF TEXAS

COUNTY OF CRANE

BEFORE ME, the undersigned, a Notary Public in and for said County and State, on this day personally appeared Bonnie V.Covill, wife of the said James E.Covill, known to me to be the person whose name is subscribed to the foregoing instrument, and having been examined by me privily and apart from her husband, and having the same fully explained to her, she, the said Bonnie V.Covill acknowledged such instrument to be her act and deed, and she declared that she had willingly signed the same for the purposes and consideration therein expressed, and that she did not wish to retract it. Give n under my hand and seal of office this 6 day of December,1947.

(SEAL)

                          A.N.Wright   A.N.WRIGHT
Notary Public in and for
Crane County, Texas

Uncle Albert
Aunt Weathes husband
(note from Sue Neely Christen, mother's sister)

July 1947–June 1950: Deeds of sale of lots by Bill Hollins

August 4, 2005: Marker dedication attendees

Notice that, in deference to Lou Young's request that he "be moved up a little on the list," we present these in reverse alphabetical order. Louie, always a thorough reporter, included city names of the out-of-town people present.

Young, Lou; Williams, La Shawn (Tyler); Williams, Blake; Williams, Blair; Webb, Patty; Vines, Mary (Lubbock); Vines, Darrell (Lubbock); Turner, Angela Boothe (League City); Tiner-Keutz, Robin; Taylor, Bud; Stroder, Evelyn; Stroder, Charles; Weatherby, Sherry; Sheppard, Nikki (Texas City); Ross, Sharon; Pierce, Phil (Phoenix); Pierce, Mary (Phoenix); Pettit, Debra Milam; Overton, Lewis;

Milam, Gloria; McFarland, Debby; Lane, Arthur; Keutz, Leroy; Jones, Louie; Jeffery; Oretha (Arlington); Jeffery, Jackie; Jeffery, Florence; Jeffery, Daisy; Jeffery, Carl (Arlington); Ifera, Sharon; Ifera, Ray; Hurst, Sara (Midland); Hurst, Rita Kuhn (Midland); Hurst, Chuck (Midland); Hayes, Georgia; Grissom, Toby (Carrolton); Grimes, Grover (Houston);

Griffin, Marsha Plummer (Granbury); Griffin, Gene (Granbury); Gilham, Clay (Canyon); Fletcher, Ryan (Houston); Fletcher, Kathleen (Gardendale); Fletcher, Glenn (Houston); Estes, Mary (Odessa); Estes, Bill (Odessa); Dawson, Bill; Davidson, Kathrin; Davenport, Jo Ann (Odessa); Cowden, Patsy (Peoria, Arizona); Cowden, Gene; Collins, Nancy Webb; Collins, Janet; Carroll, Betty (San Angelo);

Butler, Billy Pat; Bowens, H. A.; Boothe, Johnny; Boothe, Don; Bishop, Tommy (Midland); Bishop, Estiene; Basurto, Heather; Lane, Annette Lopez; Abron, Patsy; Abbott, Bill (San Angelo).

BIBLIOGRAPHY

Bishop, Estiene. "Church History." Speech at Mount Zion Church Anniversary Celebration, Crane, Texas, February 8, 2004.

Bissinger, H. G. *Friday Night Lights,"* Reading, Massachusetts: Addison Wesley Publishing Co., 1990.

———. "*Friday Night Lights,"* *Sports Illustrated* 73, September 17, 1990.

Bond, Wilson, Ruth Kindiger, and James Roberts. "Andrews, Texas: First Fifty Years." *Texas Permian Historical Association Annual 2*, 1962.

Branda, Eldon Stephen, ed. *Handbook of Texas, A Supplement, Vol. 3.* Austin, Texas: University of Texas Printing Division, 1976.

Chamales, Linda Chrane. "The Crane Wall." In *Come All you Cranes, Do You Recall ...* by Susie Hudson Marines, 203. Omaha: Self-published, 2011.

Christon, Sue Neeley. *My Times.* Stanton, Texas: Unpublished manuscript, 2013.

Frost, Robert. "Mending Wall." In *North of Boston*, by Robert Frost, 2. New York: Henry Holt and Company, 1915.

Grounds, Hazel Cristena. E-mail.

Hammerstein, Oscar, and Richard Rogers: *South Pacific.*

Hammons, Dyantha, CHS Class of 1959. "The Crane Wall." In *Come All You Cranes, Do you Recall ...* by Sue Hudson Marines, 203–04. Omaha: self-published, 2011.

Weiser, Mary Ruth. Scrapbook. Crane, Texas: unpublished, 1942, p. 2.

Keith, Karen. "Camp Kid." Unpublished essay.

Wikipedia contributors, "Detroit Wall," Wikipedia, The Free Encyclopedia. Accessed March 31, 2016. https://en.wikipedia.org/w/index.php?title=Detroit_Wall&oldid=712075000.

ABOUT THE AUTHOR

Evelyn Rossler Stroder earned a Bachelor of Arts in journalism and English from Baylor University and a Master of Arts in mass communications and American literature from the University of Texas of the Permian Basin. She taught English, journalism, and history in Corpus Christi and Crane, both in Texas. After retiring, she served four terms on the Crane Independent School District Board of Trustees.

INDEX

"Blind Men and the Elephant, The,"
    11, 49, 194, 196, 197, 205
"Grady's Gift 194
"Let America Be America
    Again" 220
Abbott, Bill 239
Abilene Christian University
    100, 156
Abron, Bucilla 15, 88, 135, 138
Abron, Patsy 239
A Farewell to Arms 127
Afro-American 49, 52, 116, 191
Airport Drive-in 54
Albuquerque 177
Allen, Joe 175
Anderegg, Dan 181, 182
Anderegg, Ricky xiv, 106
Anderson, Maxwell 207, 215
Andrews, Texas 41, 219
Angelo State University 174
Annette Lane 20, 95, 183
Annie Mae 81, 204
Atkinson, Tim 106
Austin, Texas 103, 105, 107, 108,
    121, 123, 212, 219
Barnes, Jojo 218
Basurto, Heather 23, 239
Bethune Leopards 102
Bethune School 5, 15, 21, 47, 64, 66,
    84, 89, 101, 185
Big Lake 218

Big Spring 40, 73
Bill Hollins 7, 9, 43, 73, 79, 82, 120,
    197, 239
Birmingham 195, 197, 201, 203
Birth of a Nation 117
Bishop, Donny 166
Bishop, Estiene 239, 241
Bishop, Tommy 239
Bissinger, H. G. 2
Boothe, Don 239
Boothe, Johnny 239
Bowens, H.A 239
Bowens, Rev. H.A. 15
Brown, Dorothy Abron 75, 136, 144
Buffalo Soldier 169
Burr, Jimmy 106
Butler, Billy Pat 239
Camp Kid 37
Carroll, Arlen 169
Carroll, Betty 239
Carroll, C. A. 57, 120
Carver, George Washington 111
Charleston 151
Chrane, Doug 53, 60
Christian, Herbert 18
City of Crane 23, 230
City of Odessa 180
Clark, Sir Edmund 143, 153
Collins, Janet 239
Collins, Janet (Lane) 175
Collins, Margaret 67, 188, 190, 191

Collins, Nancy Webb 239
Colorado City 102
Copeland, Larry 150
Corner Drug Store 56
Coronation of Favorites 73, 168
Corpus Christi 38, 80, 131, 195, 211
Cosby, Bill 117, 151
Cowden, Debby McFarland 15
Cowden, Gene 239
Cowden, Patsy 239
Crane Chamber of Commerce 223
Crane County 5, 23, 38, 160, 162
Crane Elementary School 149
Damron, Betty 223
Davenport Littleton, Jo Ann 107, 112, 149, 177, 189, 239
Davidson, Kathrin 239
Dawson, Bill 239
Detroit, Michigan 8, 34
Dew-Drop Inn 20, 48, 54, 56, 71, 79, 83, 176, 179, 189
Driller's Club 54
Dromgoole, William Allen 110
Ervin, DeWayne xiii, 104
Esquivel, Jessie 97
Estes, Bill 19, 103, 169, 239
Estes, Mary 239
Estiene Bishop 8, 35, 63
Fadiman, Clifton 120
Faith Baptist Church in Kermit 16
Faith in Christ 6, 65, 128, 129, 133, 134, 135, 140, 225
Faith in Christ Church 6, 65, 140, 225
FHA 5, 6, 7, 8, 45, 83, 85, 231, 232, 233, 234
Fire Department 129, 130
First Baptist Church 18, 50, 63, 128, 133, 139, 225
First United Methodist Church 140
Fletcher, Glenn xiii, 104, 239

Fletcher, Kathleen 239
Fletcher, Ryan 239
Fort Davis, Texas 156, 168, 192
Freeman, Morgan 151
Friday Night Lights 2, 90, 104
FW Kirkpatrick 219
Gibson, Cecil 52
Gilham, Clay 239
Golden Glove boxing 50
Googins, Judy Glover 49, 191
Gothard, Jack xiii, 104, 217
Graham, Texas 47, 48
Green, Dyantha 54
Green, Melissa Faye 132, 141
Greg Jones 104
Griffin, Gene 239
Griffin, Marsha Plummer 239
Grimes, Grover 239
Grissom, Toby 239
Grounds, Cris 204
Grounds, George 102
Guinn, Junior 47
Gulf Camp 46, 56
Gulf Oil Camp 46
Gulf Oil Company 41, 46, 160
Gurley, Ronnie 106
Gus Walker 9
Hamilton, Hayne xiii, 104
Hankamer, Texas 41
Harmon, Harry 49, 52
Hawkins, Carey 40
Hemingway, Ernest 127
Hemisfair 169
Highway 385 46
Hispanic 49, 52, 96, 97, 159, 172, 191
Historical Commission xii, 14, 16, 23, 223
Hollins, Argie 121
Hollins, Don 72, 120, 229
Hollins, Earnest 134
Hollins, Ernest 179

248

Huckleberry Finn 119
Hughes, Jeb 115
Hughes, Langston 220
Hunter, Madeline 112
Hurst, Chuck 239
Hurst, Mickie 23
Hurst, Rita Kuhn 239
Hurst, Sara 239
Ifera, Ray 21, 116, 157, 239
Ifera, Sharon 239
Interscholastic League Press Conference 121
Iraan 40
Jackson, Jesse 161
Jackson, Michael 166
Jackson, mISSISSIPPI 195
J. Cleo Thompson Oil Company. 11
Jeffery, Carl 239
Jeffery, Daisy 239
Jeffery, Daisy Lane 13, 136, 149
Jeffery, Florence 239
Jeffery, Jackie xiv, 21, 23, 106, 139, 239
Jeffery, Nicole 148
Jerry Grinstead 104
Jim Agnew 56
Johnson, Wayne 146
Jones, Billy Van xiii, 47, 53, 54, 95, 99, 100, 103, 104, 140, 171
Jones, B. J. 104
Jones, Eddie Dee xiii, 103
Jones, Louie xiv, 9, 13, 20, 21, 23, 63, 75, 95, 96, 97, 99, 100, 104, 106, 122, 124, 150, 152, 170, 171, 173, 174, 175, 176, 185, 189, 209, 239
Jones, Tommy ix, x, xiii, 21, 47, 53, 103, 105, 106, 217, 223, 224
jubilee 127
Keith, Karen Howard 37
Kelton, Elmer 191, 192

Keutz, Leroy 239
King, Martin Luther 85, 201
Ku Klux Klan 116
Lake Worth High School 103
Lane, Annette Lopez 170, 239
Lane, Arthur 239
Lane, Cookie 22, 66, 107, 185
Lane, Ellis 5, 13, 21, 69, 128, 135
Lane, Jack 43, 64, 152, 175, 184, 223, 224, 225
Lane, Jack and Sammi Belle 65
Last Great Westward Migration 40
Leaman, Ricky 121
Lee's Store, Texas 40
Leslie Jerome 253
Lion's Club 53
Little League 48, 49, 50, 51, 52, 94, 103, 191
Little Rock, Arkansas 202
Littleton, Jo Ann Davenport 112, 149, 189
Lopez, Juan 20
Louie, Uncle 20
Louisiana 21, 41, 42, 139
Lowery, Alice Burns 11
Magna Charta 210
Mary Ruth Speight Weiser 41
Mayes, Ed 16
McCamey 40, 64, 65, 107, 218
McFarland, Debby 239
McKay, Bob xiii, 104
McKay, Mike 97, 122
Milam, Gloria 239
Miles, Boobie 3
Miles, L. V. 3, 11, 190
Miracle, David 134
Mississippi 81, 85, 139, 151, 202, 212, 213
Modigliani 117
Morgan, David 106
Morgan, Gordon 19

Morris 47, 53, 96, 103
Morris, Elmo 19, 22
Morris, Pink 20
Morris, Thomas 121
Mosaic of Texas Cultures 100, 156
Mountain View Addition 46
Mount Zion Church 8, 15, 16, 18, 21, 35, 63, 139
My Soul Is Rested 198
NAACP 161, 162
Navarro County 39
Neal, Billy Joe 72, 98, 111, 133
Neal, Clarence xiv, 21
neal, Duffy 54, 186
Neal, Duffy 152
Neal, Terry xiv, 70, 106, 152, 156, 169
Neeley, Leon 5, 9, 43, 82
New Deal 39
New Year's Day 129, 131
New York v, 150, 197, 205
Odessa City Council 180
Odessa College 145, 146
Of Black America 117
Oil company camps 46, 55, 83
Oral History Archives 47
Overton, Lewis 239
Overton, Louis 23
Owens, Billy 106
Park Addition 6, 7, 45, 48, 65, 85, 230, 235
Patterson, Paul 191, 223
Pearl Harbor 41
Pegasus Gas Camp 49
Pena family 57
Permian High School 2
Permian Historical Society 156, 170
Permian Panthers 3, 104
Picasso, Pablo 117
Pierce, Mary 239
Pierce, Phil 239

Pink Hollins 95
Polytechnic School 149
Pony League 50, 103, 190, 191
Powell, J. Kevin 151
Praying for Sheetrock 132, 141
Professor Hall 17, 72
Purple and Gold Nuggets 57, 185
Raines, Howell 194, 196, 197, 205
Remember the Titans 101
Robbins, Jeff 43, 52, 85, 86, 99, 110, 131, 134, 139, 191, 197, 198
Robbins, Randy xiv, 52, 106
Rockport, Texas 103
Rodgers, Jill 174
Ross, Sharon 239
Safety Patrol, Crane Middle School 169
Sam Stroder 39
San Antonio 169
Saxe, Godfrey 1, 11
Seabourn, Rita 174
Sharpton, Al 161
Shelton, Lynn xiii, 104
Sheppard, Nikki 183, 239
Sixty Minutes 151
Smith, Dr. Eddy Dean 52
Smith, Jerry 171
Smith, J. L. 52
Stamford, Texas 195
Stanton, Texas 197
Stockett, Kathryn 196, 197, 198, 205
Stovall, Marshall 114
Stroder, Charles 94, 239
Stroder, Evelyn 23
Student Council 168, 177, 180, 189
Sundown Town 12
Suttles Hotel 40
Taylor, Bud 23, 239
Teague, Bill 19, 103
Teal, John 106
Tennison, L. V. 171

Texaco 49
Texas A&M 196
Texas Folklore Society 156
Texas Tech 121, 150, 162, 170, 176
Thackeray, Linda 171
The Help 196, 197, 201, 203, 205
The Wolf and the Buffalo 192
Tiananmen Square 14
Tillman, Bobby 53, 218
Tiner-Keutz, Robin 239
Tooke, Dexter 218
Turner, Angela Boothe 239
Twain, Mark 119
Upward Bound Project 176
USA Today 150
Vaughn, Gina 123
Vaughn, Tommy and Reba 63
Viet Nam 174
Vines, Darrell 239
Vines, Mary 239
Volunteer Fire Department, Crane 169
Waggoner, Mike xiii, 104
Walker 47
Wall between the Races xi, 23, 119, 195, 211
Ward, Johnny 47
Warren, Mike 171
W. D. Porch Construction 187
Weatherby, Sherry 239
Webb, Patty 20, 239
Weiser, Denzel 41, 42
White, Arlen xiv, 105, 209, 217
Wiimberley, Jannye Brown 11, 35
Williams, Blair 239
Williams, Blake 239
Williams, La Shawn 239
Williams, Mable 195, 196, 197
Willis, Ronnie xiv, 106
Wilson, Benny 106
Wink 38, 40, 58

Womack, Don 57
Women's Missionary Union 50
Wooten, Virginia 204
World War II 6, 211
Wright, Diane 168
Wright, Dr. W. T. 137
Wright, Winnie 137, 138
Young, Dennis 23
Young, Lou 21, 239

ACKNOWLEDGEMENTS AND NOTES

To list all those to whom I am indebted for the material here I might well go to the index, and then I could miss some unidentified by name, not to mention the staff at iUniverse, who showed great patience with a writer of some experience but none of it in book publishing other than annuals/yearbooks.

Hundreds of former students from my 32 years in the classroom contributed more than most will ever know. Actual quoted input for this volume began with former student Terry Neal, in a conversation in which we got acquainted as two adults. Then the first recorded conversation intended for something written started with Louie Jones and Annette Lopez Lane. They had been friends ever since their middle school years, and buddies since high school journalism days. They could discuss facts and debate opinion fairly, and that's how they helped set the tone of this account.

I will name no more names, but they would be myriad, and would include area residents who were never Crane students but had come here as adults. If you are quoted or mentioned here, or if you recognize yourself in an incident or situation in which you are not named, I thank you.

No teacher was ever more blessed.

All photos not credited here were taken by the author. Pages at the end of each chapter are allowed for the reader's own notes, whatever he/she likes. But if there is something the reader wants the author to know, whether additional info or correction, she would be glad to hear about it, at estroder1103@sbcglobal.net. Or on *Facebook*, Evelyn Stroder.

Insert, pg. _____. (re Jimmy Finley)

Jimmy didn't "rat" on who was with the group and didn't get caught, nor even identify for my record the other boys were the jail cell with him, but I had reason to believe that J. C. (?) Harmon was there. Then his son—Leslie Jerome "J-Roc" Harmon, Grammy-winner musician—recently verified that J. C. was one of them. Jerome (as I called him in school) also verified that his dad spoke of the wonderful growing up years, with specific conduct rules and very clear understanding of the penalty for crossing the line.

AUTHOR BIO

EVELYN ROSSLER STRODER EARNED A BACHELOR of Arts in journalism and English from Baylor University and a Master of Arts in mass communications and American literature from the University of Texas of the Permian Basin. She taught English, journalism, and history in Corpus Christi and Crane, both in Texas. After retiring, she served four terms on the Crane Independent School District Board of Trustees.

The author and her husband Charles M. Stroder, were honored with the naming of the Crane High School Auditorium as the Charles and Evelyn Stroder Auditorium. The ceremony took place at the All School Reunion in the summer of 2015.

Made in the USA
Coppell, TX
23 January 2022